Members of the Central Steering Group

Chairman

Miss W M Fox
Department of the Environment

Members

G J Spence
Department of Education and Science

I M Robertson
Scottish Education Department

J Kidd
Scottish Education Department

I S Dewar
Welsh Office   (to October 1974)

W P Roderick
Welsh Office   (from September 1974)

N Duncan
Arts Council   (to January 1976)

C Cooper
Arts Council   (from November 1974)

H Littlewood
Sports Council

J Palmer
Sports Council   (September 1974 to June 1975)

H Griffiths
Sports Council   (from July 1975)

P Beedle
Home Office   (to May 1975)

T A A Hart
Civil Service Department, later Home Office (to February 1975)

F N Jasper
Home Office   (from June 1974)

J H Fitch
Civil Service Department   (from June 1975)

R J S Hookway
Countryside Commission   (to July 1974)

A M H Fitton
Countryside Commission (from November 1975)

J Palmer
Department of the Environment

S Dearnley
Department of the Environment
(December 1975 to March 1976)

M B Gahagan
Department of the Environment   (from November 1976)

Consultant

Professor R Shaw
(Formerly of Keele University)   (to January 1974)

Coordinators

Miss D Dent
General co-ordinator
Department of the Environment

Dr N H Perry
Research co-ordinator
Social Science Research Council Survey Unit
later Department of the Environment

Miss A B Batty
Assistant research co-ordinator. Secretary from November 1976
Department of the Environment

Secretary

Mrs H Bowles
Department of the Environment
(to January 1975)

A H Davis
Department of the Environment
(February to October 1975)

T R Fairclough
Department of the Environment
(November 1975 to October 1976)

Preface

We were commissioned as a central steering group of officials in July 1973 to co-ordinate centrally 4 local Experiments in the development of leisure activities and to present for general publication a report of the results.

The Experiments — in Stoke-on-Trent, Sunderland, Clwyd (Deeside) and Dumbarton — were sponsored by the Department of the Environment, the Department of Education and Science, the Welsh Office and the Scottish Education Department in association with the Arts Council of Great Britain (including the Scottish and Welsh Arts Councils) and the Sports Councils. Undertaken in partnership with the local authorities and local sports and arts organisations, each Experiment had a 2-year period for action and some additional months for reporting. The first began in November 1973, the last finished in November 1976.

Soon after the Experiments started, the economy began to change for the worse and then declined sharply. This affected local programmes and to some extent restricted their scope for future expansion. We believe however that it has also highlighted one of the main lessons of the Experiments — that there is a big potential for self help in the community and that what is needed to harness it and make the best use of existing resources is not so much financial support as sympathetic and flexible relationships between public and voluntary agencies and individuals. We do not, of course, suggest that this idea is new but it is very relevant for today's problems and the Experiments have confirmed its validity.

Our report is in 2 volumes, the first containing our general report, the second the research material. In Part 1 of the first Volume, we describe the purpose and background of the Experiments, their setting up and local organisation and programmes, and seek to identify the lessons from them which may be valuable for general application. In writing up this part of our report we have drawn freely on the cumulative experience of the 4 local Experiments and the extensive research material which they provided, but in the interests of the general reader for whom this Volume is designed we have kept our use of examples, cross references and footnotes to the minimum. In Part 2 we give a fuller account of the 4 individual Experiments with brief summaries of the projects undertaken. The second Volume deals in more depth with the research background and methodology as well as with the project programmes and includes supporting material which will, we hope, be of value to practical and academic workers in the leisure field and beyond.

Records of the Experiments have been deposited centrally and locally for consultation and a film* is available illustrating some of the particular activities undertaken.

Continued

* For details see Annex 1 to Part 1, page [52]

Many people gave their time and energy unstintingly to make the Experiments possible locally. We could not hope to name them all but we would like to take this occasion to pay tribute to them and thank them, particularly the local steering groups and their teams whose efforts went far beyond the line of duty.

Table of contents

Volume 1

Summary: The Experiments and their lessons   Page   ix

Part 1: General

Setting up the Experiments   3
Background to the Experiments   3
Setting up the Experiments centrally   6
Setting up the Experiments locally   10
  Structure of Local Groups   11
  Influencing factors   12
  Determining need   13
  Local objectives and project criteria   15

Carrying through the programme   17
Information services in the Experiments   19
Transport   20
Mobile leisure facilities   21
Community theatre   21
Community festivals   23
Equipment pools   24
Projects for young people   25
Projects for the disadvantaged   27
Local outcome   28

Assessing what happened   31
Some numbers   33
Assessing organisation   33
  Local Groups and their structures   33
  Relationships with agencies   36
Using the money   38
Contact with the community   39
Support for community initiative   40
Making best use of buildings and equipment   43
Volunteers and professionals   44
The Leisure Experiments as action research   45

Leisure and the quality of life: the Experiments in retrospect   47

Annex 1 (to Part 1)   52
Arrangements for consulting centrally and locally deposited records
and for borrowing the film

Annex 2 (to Part 1)   53
Contributions to the Experiments

(

Part 2: The Experiments in action

Introduction   Page   57

The Sunderland Experiment   59
The Clwyd (Deeside) Experiment   77
The Stoke-on-Trent Experiment   95
The Dumbarton Experiment   115

Volume 2*

Contains a series of research papers on and arising from the Experiments:

Part 1: Action and research

Part 2: Selected evaluation reports

Part 3: Research papers arising from the Leisure Experiments.

* Published by HMSO

Summary
The Experiments and their lessons

The purpose of the Experiments was to see what could be achieved in 4 different urban areas by locally led campaigns to develop and increase a full range of leisure activities — cultural, recreational and sporting — a to record and learn as much as possible from the experience. They form part of a wider Government programme of action research projects designed to improve the quality of urban life.

Four Government Departments, in association with the Arts Council of Great Britain (including the Scottish and Welsh Arts Councils) and the Sports Councils, combined to invite local authorities and the appropriate arts and sports organisations to set up local steering groups and carry through a programme of local projects in a span of broadly 2 years. The areas chosen were Stoke-on-Trent, Sunderland, Clywd (Deeside) and Dumbarton. Funds were provided part centrally, part locally. Research was co-ordinated centrally, but emphasis throughout was on locally led initiative and locally developed plans.

Local Groups were set up in all 4 areas and over 400 projects mounted, many of which are continuing in one form or another. There were dissimilarities in make-up of Local Groups, approach and working methods and in the wide range of individual projects undertaken, but on the whole the Groups focused their action programmes on a relatively similar ran of activities. These were Information Services, Transport, Mobile Leisu Facilities, Community Theatre, Community Festivals, Equipment Pools, Projects for Young People and Projects for the Disadvantaged.

It was apparent that people do not necessarily see leisure needs and activities as divided between the 'arts' on the one hand and 'sports' on the other. Many projects did not fall into either category but were concerned with service to the disadvantaged and the community generally.

The main lessons of the Experiments were:

i. The potential for self help within the community and the valuable role which voluntary organisations can play, if they have good lead and are given the necessary back-up, were amply confirmed. The means needed to release this potential were shown to be relatively modest. The most important are:

   a. mutual trust, flexibility, sympathy and understanding between statutory providers and voluntary organisations:

   b. access by voluntary organisations to service and information facilities — particularly premises for meetings and use of office equipment — and to equipment pools of all kinds:

   c. access to small funds particularly by way of loan and guarantee and help with organisational and technical details of financial transactions.

ii. Local authorities can contribute in making their staff more accessible, encouraging better and more intensive use of their own buildings, in providing practical know-how and help with funding without too much red tape.

iii. People who took part were in the main already active in leisure and community pursuits. Few additional participants became involved in the time available.

iv. Little emerged to support the need for new co-ordinating organisations specially designed to plan arts, sports and general leisure activities jointly. The value of a common approach was shown to lie principally in identifying the advantages of a common service and resource centre.

v. The Experiments did not in the short time available uncover any active demand for non-traditional art forms. Well established types of entertainment appeared to be more popular although demand could be created for more innovatory forms, especially if linked with local issues. However, this required hard work and took a relatively high proportion of Experiment funds with highly variable results. It was confirmed that there is a big response to opportunities in local arts and crafts, eg. pottery, painting, local music groups, and also for loan services, eg. picture lending, cassettes, film making equipment.

vi. Local sports organisations and clubs already established appeared to be effective. Scope for further action by sports associations was primarily in the provision of services and pump priming activities.

vii. Both regional arts and sports organisations needed to overcome an impression of remoteness which they sometimes gave.

viii. On the question of widening opportunity, the experience of the Experiments varied. They seemed to confirm that for 'everyday' leisure activities a localised network of buildings and activities would suit most people's needs and wishes.

ix. Organisationally the main lesson was that an action programme is most effectively operated through a simple controlling group working closely with its professional staff and able to respond quickly to local demand. Clear division of responsibility and the establishment of sound lines of communication proved more important in practice than the particular form of structure.

x. On research methods, the system of evaluation built into the local Experiments proved practical, cheap and effective. The working methods evolved by the Local Groups and Evaluators were an important feature of the Experiments and the extent to which they were adopted by the voluntary organisations emphasise the benefits which result from the discipline of having to clarify ideas, define aims and keep progress under review.

Part 1

General

Setting up the Experiments

Background to the Experiments

1   The 4 local experiments in the development of leisure activities —
known locally as 'Quality of Life' or 'Experiments in Leisure Project' were
announced in 1973. They were conceived as part of a programme of
research into ways of improving the quality of living in urban areas. Since
1945 there had been big advances in raising everyday living standards
through the key programmes of housing, health and other social services.
However, by the mid 1960s it was apparent that there were more complex
problems which would repay study through the developing techniques of
action research where pilot action is combined with continuous assessment of its effects. A project was started in 1968, arising from the Plowden
Report 1967[1], to give priority to areas of educational deprivation. A
year later the Home Office designed a programme of community
development projects which set out to examine how the social needs of
deprived areas might be met through a closer and comprehensive co-
ordination of central and local government, voluntary organisations and
local people. Inner Area Studies were started in Lambeth, Liverpool and
Birmingham in 1972[2] to help central government through local investigation and experiment to a better understanding of the needs of inner
areas of major cities.

2   Another approach which it was thought would repay study was to
see what might be achieved by a determined drive at local level to improve some special aspect of urban living, recording and learning as much
as possible from the experience. The 4 Leisure Experiments which
are the subject of this report were the outcome. Leisure was chosen as
the field of activity not because people put it particularly high in their
scale of human values — life satisfaction studies have shown that they
attach far greater importance to homes, health and work, not to mention
family and friends — but because it is an increasingly important element
in today's world as well as being relatively easy to separate from the other
elements which go to make up quality of life as a whole. It was also a field
in which other government and local initiatives were highlighting the
need for further local action and experiment.

3   By 1973 the pattern of government support for the arts, sports and
recreation generally was well established. For a variety of reasons —
some social and traditional, some reflecting divided statutory responsibilities — artistic, cultural and educational activities had developed

---

[1] Department of Education and Science. *Children and their Primary Schools. A Report of the Central Advisory Council for Education.* HMSO 1967.

[2] Department of the Environment. *Inner Area Studies: Liverpool, Birmingham and Lambeth. Consultants' Final Reports.* HMSO June 1977.

separately from more general recreational and sporting interests. The performing arts had been promoted and encouraged by funds channelled at first through the wartime Council for the Encouragement of Music and the Arts and then through the Arts Council, established by Royal Charter in 1946. 1965 saw the publication of 'A Policy for the Arts — The First Steps'[3] and the appointment of the first Minister for the Arts. In 1967 the Arts Council of Great Britain was reconstituted; the Welsh and Scottish Arts Councils were established as committees of the Arts Council of Great Britain and by 1972 a network of Regional Arts Associations had been set up comprising representatives of local authorities and regional artistic interests. Government support for the arts in the United Kingdom has been traditionally based on 'the theory of response' as opposed to the theoretically more comprehensive 'cultural policies' adopted, though not always fully implemented, by some other countries. Grant is dependent on the twin tests of assessment of merit and the existence of a gap between expenditure and income. But did demands exist which so far had not been met by these means? The 1967 Charter had given the Arts Council its responsibility for 'the arts' instead of limiting it as formerly to 'the fine arts'. Evidence was needed on what the public wanted and whether in fact there were existing or potential new requirements at local level.

4   Government grant for sport had started as long ago as 1937 with the Physical Training and Recreation Act[4], but this was limited in scope. More general interest was aroused in 1960 by the publication of the report of Sir John Wolfenden's Committee,[5] set up by the Central Council of Physical Recreation, which called for government action and financial aid on a much wider scale. In 1963 it was announced that the Department of Education and Science in England and Wales, and the Scottish Education Department in Scotland, would grant aid voluntary organisations for sports and physical recreation and would also enlarge the provision for capital grants to local voluntary organisations. A joint circular[6] of 1964 from the Ministry of Housing and Local Government and the Department of Education and Science drew attention to the overlapping powers of local authorities to provide facilities for sport and physical recreation and asked them to review existing facilities and co-ordinate future provision bringing in specialists and voluntary organisations as required.

5   The process of central and local co-ordination and planning was carried further in January 1965 when the advisory Sports Council was set up under the chairmanship of the newly appointed Minister for Sport. One of its first measures was to establish Sports Councils for Scotland and Wales and 9 Regional Sports Councils for England. These Councils

[3] Cmnd 2601

[4] Physical Training and Recreation Act. HMSO 1937.

[5] Central Council of Physical Recreation. 'Sport and the Community; the report of the Wolfenden Committee on sport'. The Council 1960.

[6] 'Provision of Facilities for Sport'
MHLG 49/64: DES 11/64: a corresponding circular was issued by the Scottish Education Department SED 550/1964.

(which included the Northern Advisory Council for Sport and Recreation established 2 years before as part of the development drive in the North East) brought together representatives of local authorities, government departments and regional sports organisations. The administrative structure was completed in 1972 when the Sports Council was established by Royal Charter as an independent executive body, with government grant in aid, responsible for promoting sport and recreation and fostering the provision of facilities. Similar Councils were also set up in Scotland and Wales.

6   Policies had already been brought under review a year earlier. A House of Lords Select Committee was appointed in 1971 'to consider the demand for facilities for participation in sport and in the enjoyment of leisure out-of-doors and to examine what impediments may exist to the fuller use of existing facilities or the development of new ones and how they might be removed'.[7]

7   However, while arts and sports organisations had developed independently although along somewhat similar lines there was no such hard and fast division among consumers. During the late 1960s and early 1970s there had been much interest and considerable success in promoting the more intensive use of educational and local authority facilities recommended in the joint circular of 1964 of the Ministry of Housing and Local Government and Department of Education and Science to which reference has already been made. But progress had been uneven. Could a greater utilisation of existing resources be achieved by a co-ordinated effort at local level to secure integrated planning of recreational activities — cultural, educational and sporting?

8   Thus the leisure field offered both the need and the opportunity for experiment. In the 1960s attention had been concentrated on opening up a wider range of recreational opportunities in the countryside, culminating in the Countryside Act of 1968. By the 1970s, however, concern was shifting to facilities in the towns. A drive to develop activities in urban areas would give full scope for a lively local effort and might be expected to throw light on a variety of ways of stimulating local interest and leadership, encouraging participation, voluntary effort and methods of self help. Lessons so learnt could also be of value in bridging the gap which some people were coming to believe was widening between government and the governed, between 'them' and 'us'. A programme of activities was envisaged, as being more suited to short term experiment than plans involving new building.

9   It was therefore decided that 4 areas fairly remote from the influences of traditional 'metropolitan' art and leisure facilities should be selected for experiments lasting 2 years to find out the extent to which the range

[7]Two reports of the Select Committee were published in 1973 and debated in the House of Lords in 1974. The White Paper Sport and Recreation (Cmnd 6200) was issued in August 1975 and debated in the House of Commons in May and June 1977.

of existing activities could be developed and extended by a concerted drive at local level. On 24 October 1973 plans for 'an experiment in local integration of leisure facilities' were announced by the Secretary of State for the Environment in the House of Commons and by the Minister with responsibility for the Arts in similar terms in the House of Lords:

> *Much is already being done in the leisure field by Government Depart-*
> *ments, local authorities, the arts and sports councils and the Countryside*
> *Commission, to name only the most important of those concerned.*
> *However, we believe that one way to further progress may be locally-*
> *led campaigns to bring together and develop a full range of leisure*
> *resources—cultural, recreational and sporting. My noble Friend and I*
> *have therefore invited 2 local authorities in England to join with the*
> *Regional Arts Associations and the Regional Sports Councils in carrying*
> *out 2-year experiments along these lines. The aim will be to bring in as*
> *many as possible of the local organisations and interests concerned —*
> *commercial and industrial as well as public and voluntary. The selected*
> *towns are Stoke-on-Trent and Sunderland.*
> *My right hon Friends the Secretaries of State for Scotland and Wales*
> *have invited the appropriate bodies to carry out similar experiments*
> *within the west Dunbartonshire area in Scotland and the Flintshire area*
> *in Wales.[8] We hope that with the co-operation of all concerned action*
> *will start shortly. The results will be written up in a repo~ ~~~~~~~*
> *publication.[9]*

Setting up the Experiments centrally

10   The Experiments were seen from the start as a learning process in which Local Groups would carry out their own programmes of activities while the lessons to be learnt from their experience would be co-ordinated and assessed centrally. To get the best out of this it was necessary for the Experiments to take place within a common framework and for the assessment, both local and central, to be so far as possible subject to the same standards.

11   Conditions for the conduct of the Experiments were laid down with these requirements in mind. Central departments were to provide financial support and were to be responsible for the design and co-ordination of the research programme. Otherwise the emphasis was to be on locally-led initiatives and locally-developed plans. Those taking part were to be free to set up their own organisation and work out their own

---

[8]The west Dunbartonshire area comprised 5 local authorities which on reorganisation became the present Dumbarton District: it is referred to throughout this report as the Dumbarton Experiment. Flintshire, the Deeside area of North Wales, was divided on reorganisation into 2 districts of Clwyd — Delyn, and Alyn and Deeside. These became the Experiment area which is referred to throughout as Clwyd (Deeside).

[9] Parliamentary Debates 24 October 1973:
COMMONS Vol. 861. Col: 511-512   LORDS Vol. 345. Col: 737-738.

proposals, one of the objectives being to learn from the differing approaches of the various areas selected — 2 of them large industrial towns, the other 2 made up of smaller urban communities in rural settings. A period of 2 years' local action was chosen. Results were wanted as soon as possible and this was the shortest time within which measurable results might be expected; longer might have weakened the impact of what was intended to be a short-term local drive. The difficulties of mounting the Experiments during the then impending local government reorganisation were recognised but were accepted as unavoidable if results were to emerge while the reorganised authorities were adapting themselves to the powers conferred on them by the new legislation.

12   Four Departments combined to sponsor the Experiments — the Department of the Environment, which was responsible for co-ordinating the research, the Department of Education and Science, the Welsh Office and the Scottish Education Department working in association with the Arts and Sports Councils. An interdepartmental Central Steering Group of officials serviced by the Department of the Environment was set up in the summer of 1973 to develop the framework for action and research, and to be responsible for presenting the final report to Ministers. Mr Roy Shaw[10], at that time Professor of Adult Education at Keele University, was appointed part time Consultant: pressure of University business obliged him to resign early in 1974, but by then the main features of the Experiments had been settled and it was decided not to make a further appointment. Liaison between central and local steering groups was provided by a government official working with each Local Group. In Stoke-on-Trent and Sunderland they served as full members of the Group. In Clwyd (Deeside) and Dumbarton they had observer status.

13   Arrangements for financial support for the Experiments reflected their joint sponsorship. The Department of Education and Science had earmarked £200,000 a year for 2 years for the purpose, and the Arts Council agreed to make this available through the Regional Arts Associations in England and the Scottish and Welsh Arts Councils at the rate of £50,000 a year for each of the 4 Experiments. The Department of the Environment contributed a comparable sum towards the cost of staff, research and sports activities in the English Experiments, as well as helping with some of the research costs in the Welsh and Scottish Experiments and further sums were contributed by the Scottish Education Department, the Welsh Office and the Scottish and Welsh Sports Councils. The local authorities taking part contributed funds which totalled £266,000 as well as providing valuable support services.[11]

14   Since the intention was to encourage an integrated local approach, it was agreed that funds for local use should be pooled and put at the disposal of the Local Groups, who would have control over their allocation. Arrangements were also agreed in each case for the Treasurer of a sponsor-

[10] Since July 1975 Secretary General of the Arts Council
[11] Details are given in Annex 2 to Part 1, page 53

ing local authority to pay the bills and act as banking agent administering the accounts.

15 To design the research programme an Advisory Group on Research Methods was set up by the Central Steering Group with members drawn from the research sections of a number of government departments and agencies with relevant experience, not only in the leisure field. Membership of the Advisory Group is given in Volume 2. A Senior Fellow of the Social Science Research Council Survey Unit who was originally a member of the Advisory Group was later appointed Research Co-ordinator for the Experiments.

16 The research recommended by the Advisory Group had 3 components intended to:
i   obtain a clearer idea of the part leisure activities played in people's lives and the relationship between leisure and 'quality of life' in the Experiment areas by carrying out surveys both before the action period got under way and after it had ended:
ii. observe and monitor the way in which the locally established management structures of the Experiments worked in practice as an aid to the preparation of the general report:
iii. evaluate individual projects in the local programmes to derive maximum information for general use.

17 For the first part of the research, arrangements were made by the Central Steering Group for an academic survey, which had already been commissioned by the Survey Unit of the Social Science Research Council in urban areas throughout the country, to be extended in depth in Stoke-on-Trent and Sunderland. The aim was to establish whether levels of 'life satisfaction' in these 2 areas showed any significant differences from the country as a whole. The survey was carried out in late 1973 and early 1974 and the results made available to Local Groups in mid 1974. A summary of the Social Science Research Council report is at Paper 22 in Volume 2. Clwyd (Deeside) and Dumbarton made their own local arrangements for pre-Experiment surveys and the results are summarised in Papers 23 and 24 of Volume 2.

18 In the second year of the Experiments the Advisory Group reviewed their original idea for a centrally organised follow-up study after local action had finished and recommended against it for technical reasons (explained in Paper 2 of Volume 2). In Dumbarton, however, a post-Experiment survey had been commissioned as part of the local research contract with the University of Strathclyde and the fieldwork was carried out by the University's Area Survey Unit early in 1976. Paper 24 in Volume 2 relates the results of this with those of the pre-Experiment survey of 1974/75.

19 The Advisory Group recommended that the 2 other research components — the assessment of management structures and the evaluation of local projects — should be co-ordinated centrally, but organised as part of the local arrangements for carrying out the Experiments; staff appoint-

ed for the purpose should be selected and paid (where appropriate) by the Local Groups. The Advisory Group considered that integrating research with action would be more likely to encourage a realistic programme of work which would take account of the needs of both Central and Local Sponsors.

20   In assembling a body of information which would enable the local workings of the Experiments to be fully understood, (management assessment), the Advisory Group considered that it would be useful to have some independent assessment in addition to the local documentary material. They did not wish to ask Local Groups to admit a research worker to their meetings in the artificial situation of an 'observer'. Instead, arrangements were made for each Local Group to include a member called an Assessor with a suitably independent and impartial background who would be responsible for charting the Group's constitution, methods of work and progress, within a broad framework of central co-ordination. The choice of Assessors was left to the Local Groups and, in the event, each of them chose a member with professional experience in teaching or educational administration. The Assessors were given a set of guidelines on which to prepare reports, and discussed their findings on a confidential basis at quarterly meetings chaired by a Senior Principal Psychologist from the Civil Service Department who was a member both of the Central Steering Group and the Advisory Group.

21   The Advisory Group gave general advice to Local Groups on the machinery which should be established for project evaluation, laying stress on simplicity, comprehensibility and effectiveness. Since problems had arisen in other action research schemes, the Advisory Group felt it important to ensure that the main principles of project evaluation were clearly set out and understood and that the role of research staff was accepted and unambiguous. In each Experiment a social research worker was appointed by the Local Group as Project Evaluator. The Evaluator's primary task was to study the programme of projects in the local Experiments and to report on their progress and outcome to Local Groups and (through the Advisory Group and its Research Co-ordinator) to the Central Steering Group. Guarantees of the independence of the Evaluators were sought, obtained from and adhered to by all the Local Groups.

22   Since research was to be integrated into the main body of each Experiment, it was clear from the outset that Evaluators would become involved to some extent in the day-to-day activities of the Experiments. It was left to the judgment of the local Chairmen, the Evaluators themselves and the Research Co-ordinator to seek a balance which preserved the effectiveness and independence of evaluation.

23   Evaluators met quarterly as a group with the Research Co-ordinator and sometimes members of the Advisory Group, to discuss technical and methodological issues of project evaluation, and agree methods of reporting. A selection of the reports which Evaluators prepared on individual projects within the Experiments is presented as Papers 5 to 20 in Volume 2.

All reports are available for study in the library of the Department of the Environment[12].

Setting up the Experiments locally

24   The 4 Experiment areas differ in size and distribution of population. Stoke-on-Trent and Sunderland are heavily built up towns with over a quarter of a million population each, whereas Clwyd (Deeside) and Dumbarton with more rural land have smaller populations of 129,000 and 78,000 respectively, most of the people living in the scattered communities and small towns. All 4 depend mainly on industry and 3 have mining traditions. They all have a share of the typical urban problems of today including unemployment.

25   In England and Wales the new areas of local government administration became effective during the first year of the Experiments, that is in April 1974. In Scotland local government reorganisation took place a year later in May 1975. It was agreed from the start that the area boundaries for the Experiments should be those of the post reorganisation local authorities. Thus the Sunderland area was to be that of the present Metropolitan District which includes not only the county borough of Sunderland but also the growing new town of Washington and the smaller mining towns of Hetton and Houghton-le-Spring. In Scotland the Experiment area comprised the 5 local authorities now amalgamated in the Dumbarton District in Strathclyde Region. In Wales the area of the Clwyd (Deeside) Experiment comprised 2 of the 5 districts of the new county of Clwyd — Delyn Borough and the Alyn and Deeside District. In Stoke-on-Trent the boundary was not affected by reorganisation but the neighbouring town of Newcastle-under-Lyme, which traditionally has close links with Stoke-on-Trent, asked to be associated with the Experiment. This request had to be refused since it would have complicated matters after reorganisation when Newcastle was to be merged into a much larger district.

26   After preliminary informal soundings, the local authorities, sports and arts organisations in the selected areas were invited to take part in the Experiments with the following terms of reference:

To take part, in conjunction with the Department of the Environment, the Department of Education and Science, and the Scottish and Welsh Office, and in association with the appropriate bodies for the arts and sport, in a 2 year experiment designed to contribute to improving the quality of life locally by ensuring the optimum use of existing leisure facilities, cultural, recreational and sporting, and the addition of new facilities and their development so far as practicable within the period; to undertake this by means of a co-ordinated approach, bringing in the full range of local organisations and interests concerned both public and private (including industrial and commercial) and having due regard

[12] See arrangements for deposit of papers. Annex 1 to Part 1, page 52

to the spare time activities, interests and potential support of local residents; and to evaluate and report the results for inclusion in a report for general publication.

Within this broad framework it was suggested that the Local Sponsors[13] should work out their own detailed approach in consultation with the sponsoring Departments. They were asked to set up local steering groups, identify apparent deficiencies in provision for leisure activities and experiment in filling the gap with a variety of projects. It was emphasised that the Experiments were aimed primarily at developing and widening the range of recreational activities by making the optimum use of existing physical resources rather than by new building projects: that the 2-year period should be enough to allow a number of projects of differing scale and character to be carried through and evaluated: and that a measure of the success of the Experiments would be the extent to which they gave rise to a continuing programme of worthwhile activities.

Structure of Local Groups

27   In all 4 areas the local authorities played a leading role in setting up the Groups and selecting members, but different structures emerged in each area, varying in complexity, in the size and make-up of Groups, in the number of sub-groups and in functions.

28   Since it was thought there would be lessons to be learnt from their differing experiences, Local Groups were not encouraged to meet and compare notes during the early months of the Experiments though conferences to discuss matters of common interest were held centrally in the later stages. In all cases the choice of organisational structures and the design of programmes were influenced greatly by local characteristics and in one Experiment (Dumbarton) the social and geographical balance proved to be the decisive factor determining the whole structure of the Experiment[14].

29   All Local Groups included representatives of the Local Sponsors. In Clwyd (Deeside) and Dumbarton where several local authorities were concerned they comprised most of the membership. Sunderland had the highest proportion of members selected for their individual interests and experience while in Stoke-on-Trent membership was almost equally balanced between representatives of the sponsoring local authorities and representatives of the other Local Sponsors, local agencies and interests. The organisational patterns ranged from a virtually independent Group which operated almost as a trust at Sunderland; through Stoke-on-Trent and Dumbarton, where local authority forms of organisation and procedure influenced the Local Groups even though they were not directly linked to the local authority; to Clwyd (Deeside) where it was decided

[13] 'Local Sponsors' is used here and throughout the report as a collective term covering the local authorities, arts and sports organisations sponsoring each local Experiment. Details of the local authorities and organisations involved in each Experiment will be found in the individual accounts in Part 2 of this Volume.

[14] A full account of the Local Groups, their structures, sub-groups etc will be found in the accounts of the individual Experiments in Part 2 of this Volume.

with the County in the lead that the Experiment should extend and complement existing local authority activities.

30   None of the Local Groups reflected quite the wide spread of interests suggested in the original invitation to the Local Sponsors. The problems of getting limited and agreed representation for the hundreds of voluntary organisations in each area were understandably daunting and Groups used a variety of methods to involve people with a wide range of interests in organising and carrying out the Experiments. In Sunderland the Local Group, selected on an individual basis, included known leaders in the field of leisure and the Stoke-on-Trent Group included representatives of voluntary agencies and interests. Both Groups involved further volunteers in their sub-group structure. In Clwyd (Deeside) on the other hand, voluntary organisations and other interests were brought in for consultation and action, not directly with the main Group but through the Experiment officers. In Dumbarton specially constituted Neighbourhood Groups were seen from the start as the means of involving voluntary organisations and interests and given some delegated powers for the purpose, while other sub-groups were set up as necessary.

31   It had been hoped that industrial, commercial and trade union interests might also play a part in each Experiment, possibly contributing direct financial support. It was perhaps a reflection of the current economic difficulties that this latter aim was not realised in any of the 4 areas. None the less, industry and business took some part locally in all the Experiments, helping with equipment, with gifts in kind or by making staff time available.

Influencing Factors

32   As already explained, Experiment boundaries had been drawn to accord with the new local government areas after reorganisation. Less direct but equally powerful influences resulted from the changes in local authority functions brought about by reorganisation. Local authority representatives on Local Groups had to bear these in mind when considering the implications of projects for those who would be responsible for statutory provision once the Experiments were over. Some local authority members found themselves representing both present and future authorities. Reorganisation also severely limited the help which local authorities could give before April 1974. In 1 instance only — Sunderland — was a local authority officer transferred full time from the beginning. In all other instances any help given was additional to normal workload. The effects of local government reorganisation however were probably most strongly felt in Dumbarton. Reorganisation in Scotland took place a year later than in England and Wales and consequently fell halfway through the Experiment period. While the Neighbourhood Groups in the Dumbarton Experiment were unaffected by the changes, the Local Group itself (the Community Development Advisory Board) was materially reconstituted.

33 There were doubts in the early stages of all the Experiments about the conditions governing timing and expenditure. In view of the differing local situations and the need to allow time for Local Groups to complete their reporting, it was agreed that each Experiment should have its own period of 2 years for action and that the end should not be tied to a specific date. Thus the action periods varied from area to area within a span from 23 November 1973, when the Sunderland Experiment started, to 30 November 1976 when the last reports were received from the Dumbarton Experiment.

34 The local funding arrangements have been described already[15]. In considering their action programmes, however, Local Groups were concerned to know not only the total sums available to them but also whether centrally provided funds and expenditure could be held over from one financial year to the next. Carry-over arrangements were subsequently agreed but initial uncertainty played some part in determining the course of action particularly in the case of Sunderland, the first Experiment launched. Additional problems were encountered by Dumbarton after local government reorganisation, where the in-coming local authority was not committed to continuing financial support.

35 The Local Groups — consisting of people of widely differing experience and background — had to learn to work together as a team. Many were experienced in committee work but the Experiments required a new approach to leisure provision. Each Group had to identify its own purpose, find its own working methods and settle down to its own working partnership. Without exception the Local Groups felt a need early on for full-time professional staff to co-ordinate and organise the action. Where staff had to be recruited, this took time and influenced the start of an effective programme. Except in Clwyd (Deeside), Local Groups retained quite close control over day-to-day policies, although Dumbarton delegated some powers to its Neighbourhood Groups. All Experiments set up sub-groups of one sort or another to expedite business and to draw in new blood from the community.

Determining Need

36 The original invitation to local authorities and arts and sports organisations had recommended them to find out quickly, bearing in mind the emphasis on action, what gaps there were in existing provision for leisure. Major new building by local authorities was under way in the Deeside area of Clwyd (arts and theatre complex); in Sunderland (indoor sports and leisure centre) and in Stoke-on-Trent (swimming baths and planned indoor sports centre). Dunbartonshire Education Authority was in the course of providing a series of leisure centres in the area as part of a county wide scheme. Dumbarton Burgh already had a civic theatre.

[15] Paragraph 14.

37   In all 4 areas, local authorities were helping to improve existing facilities, extending others, improving services and the environment, bringing land into open space use and giving grants to local arts and sports organisations. National and regional arts and sports bodies were also giving support to selected local organisations, often in co-operation with the local authorities. It proved more difficult than expected to get a comprehensive and detailed picture of statutory leisure provision, but with their own efforts and with the help of the local authorities the Local Groups were able to get a reasonable idea of the state of play.

38   Voluntary organisations were also at work in the areas although in no case was the full extent of voluntary involvement known. Most of the local authorities were able to produce or were in the process of compiling lists of organisations in their areas. There were, however, few guides to the range of activities in which individual clubs engaged or indications of their membership capacity, or of their plans or scope for development. An early task for Local Groups was to get better information in this field.

39   They also needed to establish contact with the public, to make people generally aware that they were there and ready to listen, advise and help. The means by which this was achieved varied. One way was through the voluntary organisations (and not only those concerned with leisure) who provided an obvious and vital first link with the public both for gathering ideas and as a channel for making the Experiments more widely known. In some cases surveys of demand were mounted; in others intensive publicity campaigns were used. In the event, each Experiment evolved its own distinctive way of assessing what needs existed locally, although there were a number of common trends.

40   In general, sample surveys of people in the Experiment areas were not used by Local Groups. The exception was in Clwyd (Deeside) where a survey was specially commissioned by the Group and influenced their decisions on the structure of action. But in Dumbarton little emphasis was placed on applying the results of the survey commissioned from Strathclyde University. Similarly in Stoke-on-Trent and Sunderland, the results of the surveys by the Social Science Research Council were made available to Local Groups but little used by them.

41   All the Local Groups sought to make an initial impact through the media. Local newspapers, radio and television were contacted and a good deal of information given out in the hope of generating a wave of response from the public. The results in this were largely disappointing (though the Sunderland press were helpful), partly because interest in the media tended to focus on the sums of money available to Local Groups. This brought a number of requests for conventional grant-aiding of leisure activities, but few new ideas. Most Groups persevered with the use of press and radio publicity, Dumbarton, for example, maintaining monthly entries in 4 local newspapers.

42   The biggest effort — and probably the most fruitful in all the experiment areas — went into a large number of meetings with local voluntary

clubs and organisations. In Sunderland, almost 1,000 letters were sent and follow-up meetings were held with interested groups. In Dumbarton, the Experiment officers carried out a survey of all voluntary organisations in the district, and held a series of meetings with representatives of local interests which led to some people becoming members of Neighbourhood Groups. An exhaustive series of meetings in which almost all voluntary organisations on Deeside were contacted laid the basis for the work of Project Panels in the Clwyd (Deeside) Experiment. And an intensive round of similar meetings was carried out in Stoke-on-Trent.

43   In some of the Experiments the members of the Local Group themselves played an important part in defining local needs. This happened particularly in Sunderland where the Group quickly decided on the need for demonstration projects. They also looked closely at the effects of transport constraints on leisure participation and considered the desirability of encouraging community theatre and the possible usefulness of equipment pools. In Clwyd (Deeside), the views of Group members were influential but were themselves influenced by the results of the pre-Experiment survey, the outcome of meetings with community groups, and the balance of opinion within the operating departments of the 3 local authorities. The Local Groups in Stoke-on-Trent and Dumbarton did not take a collective view of need, but some individual members with views of their own were able to get them taken into account.

44   The action projects in the Experiments were thus derived from a number of sources. Some came about as a result of efficient lobbying by articulate local interests. Others emerged from the large numbers of contacts made by Experiment officers with a whole range of organisations. A number of projects arose from a combination of beliefs and hunches within the Local Groups themselves. Lastly, but importantly, action was stimulated spontaneously by individuals and groups who had something they wanted to do or achieve and to whom the Experiments represented an opportunity which they were quick to seize.

Local Objectives and Project Criteria

45   All the Local Groups adopted their own objectives taking into account local circumstances and needs as they saw them as well as the general terms of reference. They used these in varying degrees both as broad guidelines and as the basis from which detailed project criteria were evolved.

46   Objectives and criteria drew heavily on the overall terms of reference for the Experiments. All the Groups emphasised the need to make better use of existing resources and develop new groups and new activities; Dumbarton and Sunderland laid stress on helping co-operation between existing groups, and Stoke-on-Trent and Sunderland specifically mentioned the need to dismantle barriers between the arts and sport. Particular local criteria in Clwyd (Deeside) included the wish to help local organisations improve their activities through provision of technical advice; and

to increase public awareness of the potency of drama as a cultural force. In Dumbarton, the Local Group wanted its programme to contribute towards possible recommendations for leisure policy in the new structure of local government in Scotland. Sunderland sought to show by example the wide range of opportunities open to individuals, to increase community spirit by encouraging participation and to develop capacities for leadership in ordinary people.

47   In 3 out of the 4 Experiments the detailed criteria for the selection of projects were drawn up and applied by the officers. In Sunderland, however, both general objectives and project criteria were selected, discussed and actively applied by the Group and staff working together. They used them throughout the Experiment not only to test proposals for acceptability but also to develop ideas submitted into something more worthwhile.

48   Apart from the Clwyd (Deeside) Group which devoted the first months to planning ahead, the Groups did not settle down to draw up a programme but found themselves responding in an ad hoc way to external initiatives for projects, or considered that the intrinsic merits of a number of projects were more important than rigid adherence to general criteria. In effect, the programme criteria, with additions, became the guidelines against which project applications were judged rather than the base from which action proceeded.

49   In Clwyd (Deeside) the Local Group broadly allocated funds into 3 subject areas — Arts, Sports and Community Activities — and delegated most of the setting up of criteria for project selection to its respective sub-groups. The main Group, however, laid down the broad criteria for project selection and certain types of projects were specifically excluded — no funds were made available for the lease or purchase of land or major buildings. In Dumbarton, projects which extended the catchment area of activities or facilities were viewed favourably, as were projects with an experimental content. Sunderland, too, favoured experimentation, and projects which brought different age groups together. Stoke-on-Trent, on the other hand, was keen to give new opportunities to those groups in the community for whom leisure provision was not always adequate.

Carrying through the programme

50   More than 400 projects were mounted under the auspices of the Experiments. Between them they covered the whole range of recreational, cultural and social activities: opera and folk singing; drama and community theatre; mountain climbing and walking; film making and video; poetry and big bands; children's play and activities for older people; community festivals and symphony concerts; discovering both countryside and urban heritage; and a host of other activities. The brief review which follows could not hope to be comprehensive and should be read in the fuller context of the individual action accounts in Part 2 of this report and the more detailed project catalogues in Paper 3 of Volume 2.

51   Most projects were modest in concept and inexpensive to implement — the median cost of a project to the Experiments was around £2,000 — and since there was substantial expenditure on such items as conversions and equipment local communities will continue to derive benefit for some years to come. Because they reflected local situations and covered such a wide range of interests, it is difficult to make firm generalisations about the project programmes, but there were a number of common features.

52   All the Local Groups took the view that a balance should be kept between projects relating to arts, sport, or the community more generally. Precise balance was not possible — there tended to be more sports than arts orientated projects, because more sporting activity takes place in small teams and clubs. The smaller number of arts projects tended to be more expensive in terms of Experiment funds but this was to be expected since they included performances by professional theatre companies and orchestras.

53   The 30 or so projects which involved the Experiments in expenditure of more than £9,000 accounted for over half the total spending of the Experiments, and covered a wide range of activities. They included a number of projects which took traditional or innovative professional drama to new types of location and audience — the Victoria Theatre's Road Show in Stoke-on-Trent, the Wearabout Company in Sunderland, and the Grass Roots Company in Clwyd (Deeside). Large projects also included a Playbus and an Arts Bus; pools of equipment so that small clubs and organisations could get the benefit of fairly expensive items which they would not be able to purchase themselves; opportunities for townspeople to get greater pleasure from the countryside; low-cost conversions of older apparently redundant buildings to community leisure use; fostering amateur music-making; encouraging play schemes and lowering the cost of leisure-time transport, especially for the handicapped.

54   All 4 Local Groups were intent on a fair spread of opportunity over the whole of their areas. In the Sunderland Experiment projects were sponsored in Washington New Town and in Hetton and Houghton-le-Spring, as well as in the main built-up area of Sunderland. In Dumbarton

the structure of the Experiment itself took account of the area; groups of local people (the Neighbourhood Groups) set up as part of the Experiment and serviced by its officers brought forward and approved small projects for the Dumbarton area itself, the Helensburgh area and the Vale of Leven. The Local Goup in Stoke-on-Trent was alive to the need to spread activities throughout the 'Six Towns' of the Potteries. The Clwyd (Deeside) Experiment sought out suitable opportunities in areas of traditional culture and in new communities in urban and rural settings.

55   The extension of opportunity was also a continuing theme in the action programmes. It was linked closely with encouraging initiative from existing clubs and organisations, and helping new bodies to establish themselves. Many projects were suggested and run by volunteers, the Experiments contributing sympathy, advice, information and some modest financial help. Small grants or loans — or gifts or loans of equipment — helped many new or existing clubs to get on their feet and become self-supporting. The organisations which Local Groups devised were aimed at helping community initiative to express itself. Although more or less formal machinery had to be set up to process suggestions for projects and applications for help (except in Clwyd (Deeside) where projects were given their final shape by Panels of officials after extensive local discussions), great efforts were made to keep the actual workings of this machinery sympathetic, simple and unbureaucratic.

56   In addition, all the Experiments employed professionals of various kinds either to work on particular projects or to act as catalysts for local involvement. Actors and playleaders; community workers and poets; drama teachers and video specialists; sports coaches and visual artists — all helped to bring new experiences, develop latent interest and help along self-development in the 4 areas. Their work was sometimes controversial, occasionally unwanted by local people but was mainly much appreciated and used.

57   Some areas of concern developed spontaneously within the Local Groups and all 4 Experiments took positive steps to mount projects associated with them. The provision of information was regarded as important by all Local Groups. Access to low-cost transport was identified as a priority by the Sunderland Local Group right at the start of their discussions, and ways of providing transport were developed in all the Experiments. Linked with this was the development of 'leisure on wheels' — fitting out mobile facilities. Another venture in which each Experiment took part was the sponsorship of professional community theatre, a movement in the arts world which, at the start of 1974 when action programmes were beginning to get under way, was ripe for an extended experimental trial. Arts and community festivals were becoming popular and were also supported in all Experiments. More spontaneously (in that the stimulus of external publicity was less strong), the Experiments developed the concept of the equipment pool for individuals and voluntary bodies. This in turn was closely linked to special concern for groups of people who for one reason or another were denied the opportunities commonly available. The action programme of the Experiments developed

a number of themes which concentrated on or revealed the leisure needs of children, young people, the elderly and the handicapped. Several of these themes are dealt with in more detail in Volume 2 (Paper 4), as well as in the brief discussion below.

Information services in the Experiments

58 The improvement of information services was regarded by all Local Groups as an important part of their efforts to widen opportunity. All 4 either regularly or intermittently compiled and issued bulletins of forthcoming events, attractions and activities, and circulated them widely. The bulletins varied in style from simple leaflets to newspaper format. They were supplemented from time to time by more specialised booklets such as the 'Leisure in Retirement Guide' produced in the Stoke-on-Trent Experiment, and a number of others. In the Clwyd (Deeside) and Dumbarton Experiments, full time publicity officers were engaged by Local Groups to co-ordinate information and publicity.

59 In addition to providing information services which were aimed generally at the public, the Experiment teams in Sunderland, Stoke-on-Trent and Dumbarton looked on themselves as clearing houses for information which groups and individuals wished to exchange with each other, for example about equipment which might be available for use, teams who wanted fixtures, clubs which had vacancies, and like-minded individuals who needed a body which could bring them together to form a new club or society. This function in time merged into that of the information-and-advice centre. Some leisure organisations wanted to know how to obtain specialised teaching or coaching, or advice on technical matters associated with their particular interests. Others required help and advice on administration, finance or in dealings with statutory bodies. Although much of this advice would normally be readily available from local authorities, regional arts associations or sports councils, Experiment teams found that many local bodies preferred to come to them as 'less remote'. In some cases, Experiment officers were asked to act as intermediaries with a statutory agency. More often, however, they helped to pinpoint the appropriate person with whom contact should be made.

60 In 2 of the Experiments — Stoke-on-Trent and Sunderland — the Experiment headquarters themselves were used as information centres, clearing houses and contact points. In Dumbarton, the offices of the Neighbourhood Groups were extensively used in this way — the Dumbarton Neighbourhood Group sharing the same office as the Experiment Headquarters. As the Experiments progressed their offices often provided small but useful services for local clubs and societies — typing and duplicating, rooms for meetings, a place to store valuable or delicate equipment. The full time staff were able to act as a safety net for voluntary bodies in cases where volunteers were unable to deliver some promised service. They could also take messages and act as contact points. The development of information and resource centres was taken furthest in Sunderland,

where a Central Information Office staffed by full time receptionists was set up as 1 of the Experiment projects.

Transport

61   All Local Groups gave a good deal of thought to problems of getting people to leisure opportunities and of getting the opportunities to people. The most common need they identified was for 'on-tap' transport, not necessarily to be used by any particular group or individual on a regular basis but available quickly and in a flexible manner. The initial stimuli to action came from the particular needs of handicapped people and the elderly, who suffer from being in some respects housebound, the former because they can only travel in specially adapted vehicles, the latter because of difficulties in using public transport or organising privately hired transport. In Clwyd (Deeside), Stoke-on-Trent and Sunderland, vehicles were converted for use by severely handicapped people by adding ramps or tail-lifts or other special equipment. Conventional mini buses were available for able bodied old folk. Bookings for vehicles were normally open either to established clubs or societies or to informal groups of people. The Sunderland Experiment had one project in which an ambulance was available to take individual severely handicapped people and an escort to destinations of their choice, for example, to go shopping, to the cinema, or to visit friends and relatives. A number of people who had not left their homes for years were enabled to get about by this project.

62   Working outwards from transport for elderly and handicapped people, the Local Groups in Sunderland and Stoke-on-Trent developed more fully the idea of the community transport pool, open to all voluntary bodies and informal groups of individuals. Mini bus pool schemes worked well administratively and a very high proportion of capacity was taken up.

63   In Clwyd (Deeside) and Dumbarton, the approach to transport concentrated on bridging the gap between the real cost of leisure transport and what voluntary groups were able or willing to pay. In Dumbarton, transport grants were available to groups of people for travel to places or events, at first to destinations within Dumbarton District and later more widely. In Clwyd (Deeside) a scheme was developed to help non-car owners, especially in rural areas, to travel to cultural events. People buying tickets for the Experimental events were asked if they needed transport. On the basis of requests received, the local bus company worked out routes and laid on buses at appropriate times. Ticket buyers were given times and pick-up points. The Experiment paid for the buses, recouping some funds from a small ticket surcharge.

64   There is insufficient evidence to say whether many of the transport projects in the Experiments were fulfilling a need which could not be met by private hire firms, but there was a relatively low take-up rate for the Dumbarton transport grant scheme and the Clwyd (Deeside) special bus arrangement. The projects for transporting handicapped people, on the other hand, were very well received and indicated a gap in current pro-

vision for flexible informal travel by handicapped persons to destinations
of their own choosing.

Mobile Leisure Facilities

65   An approach to the transport question which received an extended
trial in the Experiments was that of taking leisure to the community rather
than making people travel. Included in this approach were facilities on
wheels, such as the Playbuses in Stoke-on-Trent and Sunderland; the
Sunderland Nature Bus (a travelling biology laboratory for school-
children) and the Dumbarton Arts Bus (a mobile arts workshop, cinema
and discotheque). The mobility theme also covered touring theatre, poets
workshops, travelling cinema shows and itinerant professionals who took
into the community advice and expertise in a number of fields.

66   This approach was often successful in reaching people who could not
travel because of age, infirmity or some other disadvantage and would
otherwise not have had the opportunity of seeing live arts or entertainment events, or of taking part in a number of artistic or play activities. The
use of mobile equipment, especially with community theatre companies,
allowed humble premises — church or village halls or large rooms in
residential institutions — to be used as venues for quite high quality events.
A converted 'Arts' bus which was used as a virtually self-contained 'leisure
centre' in the Dumbarton Experiment turned out to be a good way of
mopping up the energies of children in isolated housing areas. The North
Staffordshire Playbus took pre-school education into 'difficult' areas of
the city, including sites used by gypsies and other travelling families.

67   In terms of the finite and short-term funds available to the Experiments mobile facilities turned out to be expensive. Operating and repair
costs were high, and administrative backup was unexpectedly complicated, because of the work involved in scheduling publicity, bookings
and queries for a bewildering array of venues. Sometimes 4 or more
places were visited by the bus in a day. Mobile facilities drew large
numbers of users and audiences, but it is uncertain whether they were
satisfying long-term demand or whether there was a novelty effect which
might wear off. Where suitable premises exist, it seems likely that a visiting
service might achieve a similar result using a simple transport vehicle to
carry the necessary equipment instead of the more expensive conversion.
There were, however, firm indications that in some local circumstances —
remote rural areas for example or large monotonous housing estates —
mobile facilities or touring events evoked a real response, and might be an
appropriate alternative, in cost terms, to providing more permanent
facilities. The Experiments themselves could not deliver any firm conslu-
sions on this since the basis for proper comparisons of cost was lacking.

Community Theatre

68   There is lively current interest in taking drama away from its traditional setting in a theatre to project it into the settings in which people live,

work and play; and to devise dramatic forms which are based on the actual experience of audiences. Local Groups in the Experiments all took decisions to support community theatre very early on, but differed in their approaches.

69   In Clwyd (Deeside) community drama was the biggest single venture in the Experiment, and comprised 6 interrelated projects which included developing theatre-in-education, a youth theatre, technical advice and workshops for amateur companies, visiting theatre companies and a new local professional company, the Grass Roots Theatre. The impending completion of an arts centre — Theatr Clwyd — in the county town of Mold heavily influenced the style of the project. The intention was to expand and develop the drama activities organised through the County Education Department; to raise the standards of amateur production and ensure involvement at all levels of the community; and to create a receptive atmosphere in the immediate catchment area of the soon-to-be opened theatre.

70   In Stoke-on-Trent, too, the community drama project was founded on existing cultural resources, in this case the well known Victoria Theatre. With its Artistic Director as the driving force, the theatre's company of actors and technicians was augmented to develop a number of specially written entertainments and tour them in pubs, clubs, schools, halls, residential homes and hospitals in Stoke-on-Trent. Early plans to develop theatrical interests and skills in new groups in areas played by the 'Vic Road Show' did not develop, but a number of workshops were held to encourage the therapeutic use of drama in schools, hospitals and geriatric homes.

71   The Sunderland Local Group took an early interest in theatre-in-education and engaged a local north-east Live Theatre group to put on impromptu shows in Sunderland schools. It did not prove possible to put this arrangement on a longer-term basis and the Sunderland Group evolved its own company — Wearabout Theatre. This company continued the work in schools but also presented specially written plays in venues as diverse as churches and workingmen's clubs.

72   In Dumbarton, the Local Group engaged the fast-developing 7:84 Theatre, based in nearby Glasgow, to live in the District for a while, write a drama based on local history and tour it around village halls, social clubs and leisure centres in the area.

73   The technical quality of the community theatre projects set high standards in terms of rehearsal, acting, technical support and the adaptation of scripts to local circumstances. In most cases, audiences were also quite large, but the cost to the Experiment per audience member was higher for the theatre projects than for most other projects.[16]

---

[16] For general cost figures, see project catalogues in Part 2 of this Volume.

74   Surveys in Stoke-on-Trent showed that audiences for its community theatre were drawn to a large extent from the ranks of those who were already visitors to the theatre.[17] These were, however, new ventures in all the Experiment areas and it is perhaps hardly surprising that new types of activity specifically aimed at new audiences did not necessarily immediately break through to them.

Community Festivals

75   All 4 experiments supported community festivals and other events with a sharply local flavour, taking advantage of a national groundswell for types of leisure activity which mix socialising with active participation and an audience role. They found that community festivals were successful in attracting large numbers of people spanning all age and social groups.

76   In most cases where the Experiments were able to help, festivals had already been held in previous years, or groups of local people were actively engaged in planning them. In Dumbarton, the Vale of Leven Gala, and Helensburgh Week were established events before the Experiment. The Stoke-on-Trent team were involved in 7 local festivals in 1975 alone. Festivals in the Clwyd (Deeside) area at Holywell, Kelsterton and Mynydd Isa involved the active co-operation of Community Councils as well as the Experiment and individual volunteers. The involvement of Experiment officers included the active organisation of community events, including a Workingmen's Club Fete in Sunderland, and the Dumbarton Arts Festival — a 2 week programme of events to demonstrate the potential for greater use of the town's Denny Civic Theatre.

77   It was, however, more usual for the Experiments to offer help and advice to others and, where it was needed, some financial assistance guarantee. From the experiences in the 4 areas, it seemed that the most successful events were those in which local people were in charge. Things were not quite so successful where the basic organisation was done by 'outsiders', although combined efforts sometimes led to locally spectacular successes, such as the Holywell Festival in Clwyd (Deeside) and the Blurton Festival in Stoke-on-Trent.

78   If it was true that local volunteers got the biggest response from their community, it was also the experience of the Experiments that volunteer resources should not be overtaxed. The community events which made the biggest impact, including some successful Welsh culture events in Clwyd (Deeside),[18] were very concentrated in the area which they covered and, spread over the whole year, were within the capacity of the local community resources.

[17] See Paper 13 in Volume 2
[18] Notably in the Treuddyn area of Delyn: Clwyd (Deeside) projects 130 – 138.

Equipment Pools

79   Beginning with a pool of musical instruments for use by school-children in Sunderland, all the Experiments developed successful pools of equipment for loan by individuals, groups or clubs. In Clwyd (Deeside) and Dumbarton, central equipment pools were established. In Stoke-on-Trent and Sunderland, pools were set up as required to supply a range of specialised equipment. The wide range of objects and materials made available by Local Groups included, in Clwyd (Deeside), for example, marquees, bleacher seating, trestle tables, ropes, public address systems and chemical toilets — in fact, virtually everything needed to stage an outdoor event, as well as camping and mountaineering equipment. Further items included cine equipment, brass band instruments and port-able seating and staging for musical performances. The Dumbarton Central Pool of Equipment loaned out gear for a number of art and sport-ing activities — archery, athletics, ski-ing and weight training, as well as lighting, recording equipment, an electric organ and a range of necessities for outdoor events.

80   The Sunderland Experiment tried a number of interesting innova-tions in managing its equipment pools. A large stock of equipment for countryside activities was managed by a specially appointed youth leader who also played a big part in developing young people's interest in out-door pursuits at 3 mountain centres supported by the Experiment. Stage lighting equipment, for use by schools and amateur companies in the Sunderland area, was entrusted to the boys of Ryhope Comprehensive School. Management of the pool and the technical demands of maintaining the equipment made an important contribution to the skills of the boys involved and became virtually part of their education.

81   Most of the Experiments found that some management of inventory and bookings was obviously needed and occasional intervention was necessary to stop some groups monopolising equipment. But most of the equipment pools were run in a flexible manner and with easy and unfussy access. In terms of usership, all the equipment pools were undoubtedly successful. Many organisations who could not have afforded to hire specialised equipment commercially (and a number who could!) gained the benefit of enhanced facilities and events. The 2 big issues which the Experiments were not wholly able to resolve within their timespan were those of amortisation and ongoing management.

82   Within the Experiments, charging policies for equipment varied, from free or mainly subsidised use to a cost calculated to ensure replace-ment of equipment after a reasonable period of use. Local Groups gained the impression that most users were willing and able to meet charges based on the replacement principle, but effective sinking funds had not been established by the time the Experiments wound up.

83   The future of some of the pools also had a question mark over them. For many items of equipment, the local authority seemed to be the natural residuary legatee and in several cases there was no doubt that equipment

would continue to be loaned out on the 'easy access' principle embodied in the Experiments. In other cases there was at least some doubt whether equipment might not in time be absorbed into the general stores of the authority and not be as readily available as hitherto. For example, the pool of musical instruments in Sunderland was originally intended for use by children who did not normally get music lessons at school. Managed on behalf of the Experiment by the music service of the Education Authority, however, the distinction became blurred and the instruments became an additional resource for the normal music service. Similar apprehensions were felt by the Sunderland Local Group about the future of the important Outdoor Equipment Pool, but there is a good prospect of its original character being maintained through the newly established Management Trust comprising representatives from the local authority and voluntary organisations in the Borough. A management solution used in all the Experiments for large quantities of equipment bought from Experiment funds, whether for pool use or not, was to vest them formally in the local authority or another statutory agency and then let them out on permanent loan to appropriate local organisations.

Projects for Young People

84   Except in Clwyd (Deeside), where provision for play was excluded (as being a local authority function) by the Group's criteria, the Experiments put a lot of effort into projects for pre-school and primary school children. The biggest concentration of effort probably came in Stoke-on-Trent, where the Experiment sponsored the creation of a Play Council, funded the work of the North Staffordshire Playbus in Stoke-on-Trent, ran a series of 'Playmate' schemes in which paid playleaders in parks or rough sites drew in children from poorly-provided housing areas during the summer holidays; supported a project to make contact and establish bonds with a group of under-10s who seemed to be running wild in the streets of Hanley; and encouraged special childrens' events at the Gladstone Community Centre, set up in the Pottery Museum with Experiment backing.

85   The Stoke-on-Trent play projects relied to quite an extent on paid staff. The ambitious Neighbourhood Playschemes project in Sunderland which embraced 16 play schemes in 1974 and 1975 laid great emphasis on local organisation by parents and other helpers, but also found that some paid backup — as unobtrusive as possible — was required. Children's play projects in Dumbarton were on a smaller scale than in Stoke-on-Trent or Sunderland. Here, too, summer playschemes were supported and, like those in the other Experiments, were heavily used. All the play facilities supported by the Experiments were complementary to those already provided by local authorities; and in all areas the number of holiday schemes, both voluntary and local authority supported, increased over the period of the Experiments without any sign that saturation point was being reached. The Dumbarton Experiment also helped a number of Mother and Toddler Groups to place their organisation on a sound footing and to make contact with each other. A novel associated idea was a

Design-a-Toy Competition, in which the winning design was put into manufacture by a national toy firm.

86   Play activities in the Experiments were not without controversy. In Stoke-on-Trent, bad feeling among members limited the usefulness of the Play Council. There were exchanges, at times heated, between representatives of the Sunderland Neighbourhood Playschemes and the local authority officers on the question of whether the local authority fully accepted and would continue the form of organisation funded by the Experiment. And lively discussion was sparked off in Dumbarton by the Local Group's decision to give a grant to a children's club to pay a group visit to London — an apparent joyride to some but vindicated by the boost which it gave to the club's morale, organisation and fund-raising. One relative gap in the action programmes of the Experiment was in projects which related specifically to the secondary school age group and immediate school leavers. On the face of it, young people are well catered for by the education system and commercial leisure providers. On the other hand, people questioned in pre-Experiment surveys in Dumbarton, Stoke-on-Trent and Sunderland, and the school leavers surveyed in a special study by the Stoke-on-Trent Experiment team, assigned high priority to teenagers as a group for whom more should be done.[19]

87   A number of projects were, however, mounted for teenagers and those just a little younger. The Sunderland Local Group convened a Sixth form conference and set up a Youth Leisure Panel of young people to bring forward ideas for activities. Also in Sunderland, the Outdoor Activities scheme showed the undiminished potential of 'traditional' activities for harnessing the energies of young people, given the right approach and leadership. The School Leavers Survey in Stoke-on-Trent resulted in the production, by the Experiment team, of a School Leavers Leisure Guide. In Dumbarton, the leisure centres of the Youth and Community Service were already providing informal opportunities for constructive use of leisure time, especially for young people from the bleak housing estates of the Vale of Leven. A community worker funded by the Dumbarton Experiment and based in Renton added to this work. And the Experiment supported the efforts of local people in the isolated village of Rosneath to start up a social club for teenagers, run by the young people themselves.

88   However, virtually none of the project applications considered by the Local Groups came spontaneously from groups of young people. This may have partly been due to an inevitable lack of experience and assurance, or to the pre-occupation of teenagers with establishing their self-identity by reacting against what appeared to be 'establishment organisations'. Whatever the reason, where the Experiments worked specifically for young people, it was largely as a result of initiative within the Experiment teams of Local Groups.

[19] See Papers 22, 24 and 25 in Volume 2

Projects for the Disadvantaged

89 'Disadvantaged' is an often conveniently imprecise though sometimes invidious label. It is used here simply to describe projects designed for people who are ordinarily unable to avail themselves of opportunities which the majority of people regard as commonplace. In particular, the Experiments made special efforts to give old people and the physically handicapped a share of what they had to offer.

90 At the outset, 1 or 2 Local Groups hoped that it would be possible to provide elderly and handicapped people with opportunities which they could use as individuals, rather than having to rely always on membership of organised groups. In some cases this was possible. The mobile library service for the housebound in Clwyd (Deeside) provided individual attention from trained librarians. The 'talking newspapers' for which the Clwyd (Deeside) and Dumbarton Experiments provided good quality recording equipment, and tape-recorded stories for people in Dumbarton's geriatric wards, also got across to individuals. The Dial-a-Bus scheme in Sunderland was specifically designed to give severely handicapped people individual freedom of transport.

91 In the main, however, Local Groups found it so difficult to make contact with elderly or handicapped people on a individual basis that it was only sensible to work through existing organisations or, indeed, to set up new ones. Among the projects sponsored, all the Experiments donated or loaned equipment to old people's homes or geriatric hospitals — most commonly record players or tape recorders. In all the Experiments, too, community transport schemes usually sprang from the needs of elderly or handicapped people. Entertainment for people in institutions was another common theme. All the community theatre companies played in old people's homes and hospitals. In 2 of the Experiments — Stoke-on-Trent and Dumbarton — involvement went further and old people were drawn into dramatic activity through theatre workshops or impromptu improvisations. The Dumbarton Arts Bus provided a film service for several institutions and the NE Wales Film Society made similar provision in the Clwyd (Deeside) Experiment.

92 Holiday schemes were devised specifically for mentally handicapped children in Clwyd (Deeside) and for children with severe physical disabilities in Stoke-on-Trent. Because of the special problems of these children the help of their schools was indispensable but numbers of volunteers appeared, especially from the upper forms of secondary schools. Some projects sought to lessen the differences between handicapped and able-bodied people by involving them in activities together. Examples included a Riding for the Disabled scheme in Stoke-on-Trent and a PHAB Club (Physically Handicapped and Able Bodied) for young people in Sunderland.

93   An individual feature of projects for the disadvantaged in Stoke-on-Trent was the use of publicity methods to involve people. The Experiment supported educational courses on Leisure in Retirement and published a lively guide. It ran a successful 'Life Begins at 60' campaign which became a self-supporting movement of social events for old people. And, in collaboration with BBC Radio Stoke-on-Trent, the Experiment team mounted a 'Time to Care' project which had regular features on people and groups in the city who needed support.

94   Projects specifically for people whose disadvantage was poverty were fewer in number than those for young children, old people or the handicapped, although of course each of these conditions is often linked to poverty. For example, 1 of the objects of providing low-cost transport for old or handicapped people was to bring within their reach opportunities which would have been denied them by the high cost (as well as other difficulties) of securing appropriate transport. Play schemes and playbuses mostly operated in areas where spontaneous action had not yet occurred — mainly large council estates. Among projects designed to give wider opportunities to young people in areas of urban deprivation was one to provide outdoor pursuits for probationers in Clwyd (Deeside), the Hanley Youth Project in Stoke-on-Trent, and an Intermediate Treatment Centre in Dumbarton. The Experiment-funded community worker in the Vale of Leven helped an existing community action group (CARE — Community Action Renton) to establish an information shop and community newspaper and to encourage environmental improvement in a vandal-prone locality. Dumbarton's Conference on Alcoholism, which led to the formation of a Council on Alcoholism with powerful local support, was also prompted by a reaction to a form of stress which is often linked with poverty.

Local Outcome

95   By the very nature of the Experiments, the stimulus which they could provide to activities and organisations was short-term. Projects which received cash or organisational assistance (as opposed, say, to the outright gift or permanent loan of equipment) were given help for a period which did not normally exceed a year. Some were planned as one-off events or demonstration schemes and were not intended to continue. By the time support from the Experiment came to an end, some projects had become self-sufficient and were in a position to carry on by themselves. Other projects needed to rely to a greater or lesser degree on help from outside bodies. Several were taken on by local authorities, either because this had been built into the original Experimental funding, or because they had demonstrated their value and commended themselves as continuing ventures even by the searching criteria applied in a period of financial stringency. Some projects, including several high-cost ones, inevitably fell victim to the economic circumstances of the times. Others did not prove their worth sufficiently to justify a continuing commit-

ment.[20] Time will show how far the action programmes have added to the long-term structure of leisure opportunities in the 4 areas. A roll-call at the end of the action period indicated, however, that a majority of the projects sponsored by Local Groups were relatively assured of a continuing future.

[20] Projects which exemplify each of these outcomes in turn are: Amateur Academics, Sunderland project no.1; Denny Arts Festival, Dumbarton project no.64; New Guitar Society, Clwyd (Deeside) project no.103; Islamic Centre, Stoke-on-Trent project no.21; Burslem Leisure Centre, Stoke-on-Trent project no.4; Outdoor Activities Co-ordinator, part of Sunderland project no.24; Dumbarton Community Newspaper, Dumbarton project no.58.

Assessing what happened

96 'The money was well spent' . . . 'extremely successful and worth-while' . . . 'some lasting benefits' . . . 'local people will not see any difference at all' . . . 'fantastic return from the combination of public and voluntary agencies' . . . 'most interesting, many lessons learnt' . . . 'it was misconceived in concept, projects ill chosen, the money could have been been better invested elsewhere' . . . 'money was squandered in certain areas' . . . 'considerable success though not wholly in the direction hoped for' . . . 'given a new dimension' . . . 'particular achievement not from the money spent but from the activity generated, the exchange of information, improved communications and identification of latent needs' . . . 'some significant national spin off'. These were among the wide range of comments — many favourable, a few highly critical — expressed by Local Sponsors and members of Local Groups whose views were canvassed when the Experiments were wound up.

97 More general local reactions were not easy to assess. Clubs, societies, communities or individuals who had been helped thought highly of the results. Others, whose suggestions had not been followed up, felt 'that the Experiment was not for them'. People who had not heard about particular events — or if they had, did not associate them with the Experiments — were critical about publicity. A number of people thought that projects tended to favour elitist acitivites, other that there was too much concentration on the way-out and off-beat. Some young people felt that no one wanted to help them, while others who had been helped were enthusiastically grateful.

98 Measured in terms of activities undertaken, the record is however impressive. Within a very short time — the period of intensive action being mostly little more than a year — the Local Groups mounted and carried through varied and colourful programmes of projects. Many of these projects were to be continued in one form or another, a test which had been accepted as a hallmark of success in the early stages of the Experiment and which must rate even more highly in the present very difficult economic circumstances. An assessment made from the Evaluators' reports of an 'achievement factor' in the local projects indicates a success rating of about two-thirds. As Paper 4 of Volume 2 suggests, this is 'indeed respectable'. True, there had also been problems — some of management due to inexperience or clashes of personality, others to failure to appreciate the true objectives of the Experiments. Working within a tight span limited the period of action and cut down the time, sometimes vital, for preparing, negotiating and mounting projects. Some projects failed, some were stillborn. Yet others including some of the most promising had made little more than a start when the Experiments came to an end so that it was impossible to assess their long term value.

99 In reviewing the Experiments as a whole, however, their local impact, important though it was, is only part of the story. From the beginning the local action programme had been seen by the Central Sponsors as a source

of ideas and lessons for the benefit of others considering similar activities in the future. To what extent had these hopes been realised? Had the Experiments proved their worth in terms of the lessons to be gleaned?

100   There was a wealth of material available for the purpose — the Local Group papers and reports, the reports of the Management Assessors, the project evaluation reports and the Dumbarton survey. With all this and with the help of discussions held towards the end of the Experiments with the local Chairmen and Directors, with the Assessors and with the Evaluators, it has been possible to build up a rich picture of the extent to which the Experiments penetrated the fabric of local life. It covers the Local Groups' experience in organising the project programmes, the interest and participation stimulated by the Experiments, the extent to which existing and new demands could be identified in the areas and the degree to which action set in train by the Experiments seemed likely to continue beyond the period of their first impulse. It has been possible to identify a number of useful lessons, which while not necessarily new are supported by a variety of evidence. The objective reports of the Evaluators have been particularly valuable in this and extensive use has been made of a co-ordinated study of their reports carried out centrally with their help.[21]

101   Not all the lessons carry the same weight. At the best, only 4 areas were involved and some of the characteristics they have in common would not necessarily be so dominant elsewhere. But some findings are so strongly supported by evidence from all the 4 Experiments that they must be taken as of general application. Others with less overall support would seem indications rather than positive findings. And lastly there are some which pose questions rather than answer them since the evidence on which they are based is inconclusive, even conflicting — but which none the less are included for their value in provoking thought or stimulating further experiment.

102   How to present the results with so much material available was something of a question. Some lessons of wider than local application have already been hinted at in the previous section — the importance of local initiative; good results from backing enthusiasts and the value of common services provided by the Local Groups for this purpose; the attention which should be paid to publicity; the need to be realistic about the costs of some types of venture; the success of equipment pools, the potential of mobile facilities in appropriate circumstances. They will be referred to again in this section along with lessons which arise from the general operation of the Experiments as well as from specific projects. In the event it seemed best to give the lessons not in any preconceived framework but in the sequence which flowed naturally from the course of the Experiments themselves.

21 The bulk of Paper 4 in Volume 2 is drawn from Evaluation Reports on projects.

Some numbers

103   Even where sources are utterly reliable and methods of collection impeccable, numbers can be troublesome to handle and interpret. It must therefore be readily admitted that any attempts to quantify the Leisure Experiments are by the highest standards of evidence less than usually reliable. Figures through which to summarise the local effects of the Experiments have not been easy to come by. By their very nature, projects were locally-based, operated informally and involved people at different levels of intensity. Rigorous head counting (which in any case only tells part of the story) was not appropriate to many of the activities in the Experiments. But some quantitative indicators to underpin other evidence are indispensable and broad estimates have been made of the orders of magnitude at which local people were touched by or became involved in their local Experiments. In very rounded terms the number of people directly involved in Experiment projects was well over a quarter of a million (40,000 in Clwyd (Deeside), 80,000 in Dumbarton, 90,000 in Stoke-on-Trent and 80,000 in Sunderland). When an allowance is made for the fact that many activities continued over a period of time the number of 'person/sessions' in the Experiments — broadly speaking the number of people involved multiplied by the number of times they took part in activities — has been estimated at 900,000 (135,000 in Clwyd (Deeside), 225,000 in Dumbarton, 255,000 in Stoke-on-Trent and 285,000 in Sunderland). It should be stressed that the figures are extremely crude estimates and are intended only as a guide to levels of participation. A fair proportion of the numbers in all the Experiments were made up of audiences for relatively traditional forms of entertainment, and this should be taken into account when interpreting 'involvement'.

Assessing Organisation

Local Groups and their Structures

104   Experience of the Local Groups suggests that an action programme is most effectively operated through a simple, well integrated structure which can react quickly and flexibly to the demands made on it. The relatively small and independent Local Group in Sunderland meeting frequently (fortnightly) and with Group members and officers working together as a team, perhaps came nearest to achieving this, though Clwyd (Deeside), where wide powers of action were delegated to officers with the full backing of local authority departments, showed just how effective a service can be when operated by sympathetic and committed local authorities. Dumbarton, which had the most complex structure, probably experienced the most difficulties, while in Stoke-on-Trent, local authority and other interests were sometimes in deadlock on controversial issues.

105   Each of the Groups discovered very quickly that it could not hope to deal directly with all that was involved in running the Experiments, and set up sub-groups and working parties to advise, to contribute ideas, and to co-ordinate. In Dumbarton, Neighbourhood Groups were set up at

the beginning of the Experiment and exercised their powers of decision delegated by the Local Group. In practice the particular mix of sub-groups and the division of responsibilities between them appeared less important for effective action than ensuring that their responsibilities were clearly defined and understood by all concerned and their lines of communication with the parent Groups clearly laid down and recognised.

106   All the Groups found that they needed to engage professional staff but, as with the sub-structures they adopted, the size and build up of the professional team and the division of responsibility between them and the Local Group they served proved to matter less in practice than a clear understanding about division of responsibility and the establishment of sound lines of communication. Undoubtedly free discussion and frank interchange of views between Group members and professional staff contributed greatly to success in those Groups where these were features of the organisation. Naturally enough, in view of the relatively short action period, it was an advantage where the professional staff started with a knowledge and understanding of the area. Even so, this proved of second-ary importance to enthusiasm for and appreciation of the purpose of the Experiments. All the professional staff had this in common.

107   The short action period was a common item of complaint from Local Groups, although all of them also recognised the virtues of concentrating effort into a relatively brief period of time. It is interesting to note how the different groups reacted to the time constraint. The Sunderland Group launched rapidly into a number of projects and committed virtually all its funds in the first full year of the Experiment. It then spent the second year filling in gaps so far as its means allowed, evaluating and weighing up the progress of projects and seeking to tie them into an ongoing frame-work. In contrast, the Local Group in Clwyd (Deeside) felt that a gestation period was necessary, however short the Experiment period. They allowed several months for thinking, planning and gathering in the views of many disparate organisations. This no doubt reflected the natural contrast between an independent innovatory body which needs first to make a strong impression and then to consolidate its gains; and a local authority based organisation, which can from the outset plan how to blend in its activities with the longer-term programmes of the authority. But both the 'learn-as-you-go' approach and the 'get the plans right first' approach provided valuable insights into different but legitimate ways of organising a programme of action.

108   None of the 4 areas kept the existing Group and sub-group structure going after the action phase ended. Bearing in mind the one-off nature of the Experiments and the economic climate of the day, this can scarcely be taken as conclusive evidence one way or another of the long term value of the Groups. But 1 objective of the Experiments was certainly to test what more could be achieved by getting arts, sports, local authorities and other interests to work together for a common end. Apart from possible practical gains from joint planning, were there also less tangible benefits to be derived from what was spoken of at the time as a 'cultural synthesis'?

109   Little emerged from the Experiments to suggest that the integrated

approach led to any significant cross fertilisation of ideas. A few events were planned deliberately to bring arts and sports activities together, such as festivals of music and movement in Clwyd (Deeside) and Dumbarton. These were highly successful examples of their kind but were planned and enjoyed as one-off events which demonstrated the concentration and dedication required to achieve high standards of performance in physical co-ordination — whether in athletics, gymnastics or dance. A longer term effect of the integrated approach was the sense of community responsibility, particularly towards housebound and disadvantaged people, which all the Groups manifested. It is difficult to avoid concluding, however, that this resulted less from bringing arts, sports and other recreational interests together, than from people of goodwill getting round a table to discuss how best to widen opportunities for all.

110 Individual members of Local Groups confirmed that the experience of working together was valuable and they found gain in exchanging views and getting increased understanding of each other's problems. Nevertheless all the Groups dealt with arts and sports activities in different subgroups and/or panels which evolved their own programmes and developed their own projects. Only in provision for the handicapped did joint planning prove of special value, and this was primarily because of the practical problems involved — for example, provision and adaptation where necessary of special transport.

111 Clearly then, people drew their own lines of demarcation between what they thought of as arts and what they thought of as sports and projects and events were in most areas organised effectively along established lines. Where a combined approach did prove of significant value was in the provision of common services which were useful to 'organisations' rather than specifically to arts or sports 'activities'. The success with which most of the Groups acted as a general resource centre and backup agency was greatly helped by their independence, their ability to function over a wide range of activities and to respond quickly to need whether for funds or for information and advice. In particular their accessibility proved a major asset — both because of their status as independent organisations and because they took pains to site their offices where they could be easily reached. Though they continued to operate from the local authority base, the Clwyd (Deeside) Group recognised this too and sought to provide for a similar ease of approach.

112 Links between voluntary bodies and the providing agencies did of course already exist where there were local sports or arts councils in the Experiment areas. Even so, the Groups' experience suggested there is a demand which is still not fully met for a broad based service centre where people with new ideas or organisations wishing to expand can go for help and advice, hold meetings and keep their records and equipment. The development of the Groups' role in meeting this demand was one of the most interesting lessons of the Experiments.

113 Other practical benefits resulting from the integrated approach were seen not directly from the work of the Local Groups themselves but

in its results at local neighbourhood level — for example, in establishing neighbourhood groups to arrange the multi-use of buildings. This however was more a matter of bringing consumers together than integrating arts and sports.

114   There is no doubt that much of what was achieved was due to enthusiastic leadership at different levels (both within the Local Groups and with other organisations). The best results not surprisingly came when these people were in one way or another occupying key positions — as chairmen of a Group or sub-group, as Director, as an initiator of a particular activity. Indeed, in at least one of the Groups it came to be accepted that in selecting projects what really mattered was a leader with knowledge, drive and the ability to inspire others. But equally it was evident both in the experience of the Groups themselves and the voluntary organisations which they assisted that not only was initial leadership required but the willingness and ability to build up a support organisation with sound methods and to keep it running systematically.

Relationships with Agencies

115   In all instances a key factor which emerged very early was the importance of the Local Groups' relationships with the local authorities in whose areas they were operating. This was scarcely surprising considering how deeply the authorities were involved in the Experiments as local sponsors generously contributing not merely finance but also staff and support services. In practice, the relationship developed in 2 ways, through direct representation by the authorities on the Local Groups and in their more general role as providers of statutory services. In Clwyd (Deeside) where the local authorities themselves were responsible for initiating and operating the Experiment, these 2 functions were complementary. With the other 3 Groups however, the dual nature of the relationship in itself sometimes led to problems.

116   Despite the backing and support given in varying degrees by the authorities, all these 3 Local Groups at one time or another experienced difficulties and tensions in their relationships. These were due to a variety of reasons, some local and ephemeral, some more deeply seated. One consequence of reorganisation was that in some areas changes in council members and officers, unforeseen when the Experiments were first discussed locally, brought in newcomers who proved less co-operative than their predecessors either because of pressure of other preoccupations or because they personally lacked sympathy with the concept of the Experiments. Another source of difficulty was the one-off character of the Experiments. Some members and officers responded with imagination and flexibility to the challenge they presented but others viewed the often freewheeling methods of the Groups as something of an irrelevance to their own statutory responsibilities and established methods. And though the funds at the disposal of Local Groups were relatively small compared with the revenue resources of most of the local authorities concerned, their existence was not unnaturally resented by some local authority

members and staff at a time when local government budgets were under-going substantial pruning.

117   Difficulties were not always eased by the presence of local authority representatives (whether members or officers) on the Local Groups although this might have been expected to ensure smooth working and provide a co-ordinating link with the local authority. Some indeed gave yeoman service but others had little idea of contributing to an easy-running relationship. On occasion they functioned primarily as independent and individual members of the Local Groups irrespective of local authority links. More often, however, their thinking tended to be dominated by their commitment to local authority policies and procedures. Either way their presence on the Groups, valuable though it may have been in other directions, did not necessarily provide for effective communication with the authorities.

118   Nor did the Experiment staff always find it easy to establish working relationships with local authority officers. No doubt want of experience among some of the staff was a contributing cause, and certainly an impor-tant factor was the need to negotiate with a number of local authority departments rather than a single unit. On the other hand difficulties were by no means the rule. Some departments and officers were unfailingly helpful. In other instances where there were tensions initially, good working relationships were evolved in time, even though elsewhere relations continued to be strained.

119   The difficulties experienced on occasion showed that it is possible for organisations working in the local authority field of responsibilities to carry on without their active co-operation though it is of course very much easier with it. Direct representation of the authority on an outside organisation can be valuable but is not necessarily the best or only way of ensuring co-operation. Where there is representation, the experience of the Experiments suggests that the responsibilities of the representative need to be well thought out and defined in advance. Whatever method of liaison is adopted, however, it is important that the arrangements should be laid down clearly, that there should be co-ordination between the various departments concerned and that the individual members and staff of authorities should be encouraged to respond with imagination and flexibility to enterprises to which the authority has committed itself.

120   With arts and sports organisations and other voluntary agencies, relationships generally were co-operative. Regional Arts Associations and Sports Councils in England and the Arts and Sports Councils in Scotland and Wales were directly represented on Local Groups by virtue of their status as local sponsors whereas Local Groups differed, as already described, in their ways of bringing in voluntary organisations. Sports Council representatives in particular were able to contribute a good deal personally from their knowledge and experience. They were perhaps helped in this in the 2 English Experiments because they were not direct-ly involved in providing Experiment funds. Members representing arts organisations were naturally more conscious that, although Experiment

funds were additional to normal allocations, interests outside the Experiment areas would judge spending in the light of the limited local funds ordinarily available for the arts. As might be expected, personalities played their part: it was noteworthy in 1 or 2 instances that a change of representative on a Local Group led to the parent agency taking a far more constructive interest in the Experiment.

121   With voluntary agencies the Groups' relationships were 2-fold: voluntary agencies helped with the Experiments and were helped by them. Both these relationships provided evidence of the Groups' value as an independent organisation able to act as a service and information agency and to bridge the gap between voluntary organisations and other agencies and between voluntary organisations themselves.

122   All the Groups, irrespective of their different forms of approach, quickly discovered the need to evolve a working system which included determining objectives and laying down criteria. They were not all equally successful in working to their declared objectives but it was noteworthy that where this was done with understanding and applied in practice, the level of achievement was significantly raised. The evaluation methods built into the Experiments have already been outlined briefly,[22] and are discussed in detail in Paper 2 of Volume 2. Where evaluation became an integral part of the system and there was feed-back while action was in progress, this proved of particular value to Local Groups.

123   Voluntary bodies and individuals developing new projects in the course of the Experiments found that in this respect their experience followed that of the main Groups. They benefited, as did existing organisations expanding activities with the help of the Groups, from the discipline of having to clarify their ideas, define their aims and keep their own progress under critical review.

Using the Money

124   Handling sums of money of the order involved was a big responsibility for the Local Groups especially in a limited period of time. It was natural perhaps that many people, especially at the start, looked on their local Experiment as another grant giving agency — particularly since as already mentioned press publicity tended to feature the amounts involved as local handouts rather than as seedcorn for experimental activity. Some independent members of Local Groups with no experience of handling public funds tended to be impatient of systematised control and accounting, while some local authority members took time to adjust to the more flexible methods appropriate to an experiment. However, all the Local Groups evolved their own methods of giving support combining elements of firmness and flexibility with high standards of accountability. What was learnt on the way was the importance of getting applicants for

[22] Paragraphs 21-23.

grants to clarify their aims and, in contrast to many grant procedures, evolving a system for follow-up. Clubs and individuals responded well to this approach. The continued interest which Local Groups took in their progress encouraged people to make greater efforts to think about self-help and making do and to learn from their mistakes. Moreover, organisations and individuals became more aware of the true cost of many leisure activities.

125   In the event the amount of money provided for use by Local Groups proved far less important in achieving developments in leisure activities than the way in which it was handled. The programmes of action included some projects where expenditure was high in terms of the funds available to Local Groups, such as community theatre where professional people were specially engaged; those involving the purchase and conversion of vehicles for specialised use; and those in which buildings were adapted to provide information/resource and leisure centres. But most projects involved relatively small amounts and the help given was not always financial. It could be in kind. All 4 Experiments proved time and again that a small amount of money could give a psychological boost to existing clubs and greatly help in forming new ones: that it was often enough to give a loan or a guarantee and that giving help once did not mean that it need be repeated.

126   Experience showed that voluntary agencies responded well to trust and could administer public funds to high standards provided accountability could be combined with flexibility. Because of the overall terms of reference the experience of Local Groups did not extend to managing capital expenditure other than for adaptations and conversions, though some of these were substantial, nor to running a combined operation with other funding agencies. Nevertheless, an encouraging start was made in experimenting with forms of management in which responsibility was shared between local authorities and voluntary organisations and there is some evidence that this type of organisation functioned best where voluntary representation was in the majority.[23]

Contact with the Community

127   In each Experiment a good deal of effort was put into attempts to get more people from a wider variety of backgrounds to take part in leisure activities, to get the message of the Experiments and the opportunity to become involved across to all groups in the areas. The methods used included direct contact with organised groups, questionnaire surveys of specific age groups, organised publicity campaigns and use of press, radio and television.

128   A number of lessons were learned in these ventures. The first was

[23] For example in the Sunderland Outdoor Activities projects nos. 24-27, Stoke-on-Trent Community Transport project no. 13

the importance of publicity and information in a programme of action, and the need to see if it is getting to the people for whom it is intended. In most cases early mistaken impressions about the character of the Experiments were corrected, but the Local Groups still had to face the basic dilemma of whether their efforts in the field of publicity should be 'information' orientated or 'marketing' orientated. In general, they tended towards the first approach, but the opinion was voiced locally in some of the areas that 'better marketing' of what the Experiments could offer might have evoked a stronger response.

129   Information about the Experiments took some time to diffuse and its early impact was greatest for articulate and informed groups and individuals who were able to seek out information that could benefit them. Although intended to reach all sections of the community, publicity tended to follow established channels and, by the time the Experiments ended, participation had not really stretched to any significant extent to groups regarded as 'recreationally deprived', a striking exception being the handicapped. All 4 Evaluators thought there were signs of a 'second wave' of interest towards the end of the Experiment period among groups and individuals who had not been involved in early activities, and in the Evaluators' opinion more focussed publicity campaigns could well have brought some of this interest forward sooner.

130   In working terms, the most effective way initially of spreading news about the Experiments and their activities was to hold informal meetings with a variety of local voluntary bodies and to let word of mouth do the rest. Once established, it was found, as already described, that the most successful way of maintaining contact with the community was to develop the headquarters offices of the Experiment team as information centres. Sometimes by design, sometimes almost by accident, the offices became clearing houses for information on leisure activities. Dealing with telephone or personal enquiries, Experiment officers spread information on the location and nature of clubs and facilities to potential members or users; helped clubs to find premises; encouraged the sharing of resources; provided accommodation for meetings; and generally acted as a lubricant to the working together of a myriad of small clubs, societies and organisations.

131   While the Experiments, in their short time span, were not able to make contact with all sections of the community they did enough to highlight a number of approaches in which longer term development would be promising — the development of information and resource centres; specialised surveys leading to quick follow-up action; intelligent use of local press and radio; and sensitive use of professional organisers.

Support for Community Initiative

132   Making contact with the community was, of course, in part a preliminary step to harnessing its resources. In sponsoring a widely varied

series of projects, all 4 Local Groups found untapped pools of volunteer effort, often concentrated around a few key persons but spreading into a wide movement for community self help.

133   On the evidence of the Experiments, trust, support and flexibility are needed if community initiative is to be harnessed successfully by statutory agencies. In the matter of trust, for example, the procedures and controls relating to the use of Experiment funds were, as has been noted above, generally more informal than those used by local authorities. Yet in no cases was the trust of Local Groups abused by local voluntary groups and societies. The Experiments offer evidence that accountability for and control of public funds can be achieved without using procedures which discourage the very initiative they are intended to support.

134   Flexibility in supporting community initiative can be as important as 'getting it right first time'. A feature of the Experiments which Local Groups considered of special value was the 'freedom to fail' without recrimination but with some analysis of why things had turned out a particular way. Another aspect of flexibility is the manner in which resources are used. From this point of view, the best way found in the Experiments to harness community initiative was to provide some back-up for voluntary organisation by providing items of essential equipment or by underwriting some of their costs.

135   In terms of support, projects which were based upon existing organisations with a stable administrative structure and a knowledge of how 'the system' works were in the main more successful than those administered by 'first-time' organisations. This should not be taken as an argument against supporting new groups. It is probably inevitable that new organisations take time to find their feet, but all organisations were new once. And where new groups were given some administrative back-up, they often worked very effectively almost from the beginning.

136   In general, the Experiments showed again, if demonstration were needed, that the multitude of small clubs and societies provide an important basis of local life. Although Local Groups did not find much expressed demand for professional workers from statutory agencies to give a lead in the leisure field, there was a good deal of agreement on the need for the unobtrusive helping hand. This could take the form of advising groups on the best way to develop the administrative and advocacy skills they needed to handle their affairs effectively and put their case persuasively to support agencies; or being available to provide or obtain technical advice on, say, running a play group. The most pressing need for many small clubs without office workers among their membership was access to typewriters and duplicating machines. The idea of a 'resource centre' for Local Groups, in which access to office machines could be combined with an information service, grew naturally from the work of several Experiments.

137   It is clear that local authorities are well placed to offer unobtrusive help. There are in any case great advantages to be gained from creating a

sympathetic and responsive environment for voluntary groups, clubs and societies. Responses found to work in the Experiments ranged from small loans available quickly for an (eventually) self-financing fund; to help with minor but important problems which afflict local clubs: insurance and maintenance of vehicles and equipment; planning regulations; and discussions with the police on crowd control or the use of public highways. On the evidence of the Experiments, some changes in the organisation of the relevant departments and procedures of local authorities might be helpful. At present, the professional structures of many local authority leisure and recreation departments are organised to deliver services initiated by the authority. There may be a need to adapt organisation to back up voluntary effort more — to become less initiatory and more responsive. Keeping more in touch with groups to whom grants are made helps them to keep within the framework of the objectives which underlie the grant and sustains financial accountability while the groups appreciate the interest which is taken in them. The administrative systems evolved by all 4 Leisure Experiments were largely successful in maximising interest and contact while minimising red tape.

138   Since several Experiment projects were ventures which could hope to get support from funding bodies in the arts or sports fields, the benefits of better follow-up and support for voluntary effort apply as much to other statutory agencies as to local authorities. One particular difficulty reported in the Experiments was in getting rapid informal contact between new arts or sports groups and the regional agency based in another town. In some cases, the Experiment team acted as go-between, and the need for a more visible local presence by regional bodies was stressed. One response, tried out in Stoke-on-Trent (and Newcastle-under-Lyme) under joint funding from the Experiment and West Midlands Arts, was the appointment of an Area Arts Officer to stimulate initiative and to co-ordinate effort in the arts field. Other responses included setting up local co-ordinating bodies with good links to the regional agency — a local sports council and an arts working group in Dumbarton, a theatre interest group in Clwyd (Deeside), and a local sports council for the Alyn and Deeside District.

139   One lesson from the Experiments was that 'umbrella organisations' which Local Groups encouraged in several areas (with the aim of bringing together and co-ordinating the activities of a number of groups with similar interests and presenting a common front to external agencies) were by and large not very successful. Local authorities and statutory bodies find it convenient to deal with umbrella organisations but the extent to which they can become or remain truly representative falls off quite quickly, as individual members or groups reassert their own interests.

140   Behind the efforts of the Experiments to set up umbrella organisations was a feeling, stimulated by the original terms of reference of the Experiments, that better co-ordination was needed in the leisure field. As mentioned above,[24] there has been relatively little evidence from the

[24] Paragraphs 108 – 113.

Experiments that barriers, real or imagined, within and between sport and the arts pose genuine problems. If there is a need for a new kind of organisation, it would be for the kind of resource centre and back-up agency provided by the Local Groups which could act as a contact and mediator between the local authority and other agencies and the individual voluntary organisations. Some equivalent of local councils of voluntary service, a 'Council of Leisure Service' was mentioned at the end of the Sunderland Experiment. Such a body could be independent of the local authority though it would possibly need to look to it for support. It could suit the convenience of agencies, giving them 1 body in an area with which to discuss issues; it could provide a more flexible and less bureaucratic body for voluntary groups to deal with; and by encouraging community self-help it could point the way for a more effective deployment of local authority recreation staff, either at existing or lower levels of staffing. There were signs, at the end of the Clwyd (Deeside) Experiment, that with the encouragement of County and District Councils, the statutory Community Councils (established when local government in Wales was reorganised) were coming forward to take up a grass-roots co-ordinating activity.

Making best use of buildings and equipment

141   The action programmes of the Experiments showed that there is considerable scope for increasing the effective use of resources already in the leisure field or potentially available to it. The Experiments demonstrated how more flexible use of existing buildings could increase their contribution. They showed how old buildings could be put to new use; and how a good deal of short-term benefit could be got from intelligent use of temporary buildings.

142   Local Groups faced with a specific hindrance to the more intensive use of publicly-owned facilities were often able to suggest a sensible and practical way of overcoming the difficulty. Psychological obstacles seemed to be as important as concrete ones in preventing the better use of facilities. The initial breakthrough into more intensive use was important. Once the practicability of, for example, sharing a facility between different groups was demonstrated, hitherto 'insuperable' problems became manageable.[25]

143   This is not to say that obstacles to more intensive use do not genuinely exist. There are problems in staffing arrangements, especially where unsocial hours and overtime claims are involved. Well over a decade since the Joint Circular on Dual Use of Educational Buildings[26] the Experiments have indicated that there are still difficulties for local education authorities in following through the logic of developing schools as potential centres for the whole community. Local authority departments and other organ-

---

[25] See, for example, Multi-Use of Local Authority Premises project, Sunderland (Paper 17 in Volume 2).
[26] See footnote 6, page 4.

isations tend to feel possessive about 'their' buildings and facilities. Sometimes this is overt, at others masked by (real or exaggerated) fears of damage to equipment or premises. The Experiments did not invariably overcome these obstacles successfully, but there was enough to demonstrate that a determined approach to them could be effective.

144   Better use of human resources is as important as the use of physical resources and, not surprisingly, the first can often lead to the second. In addition to the evidence from several Experiment projects that conversion and adaptation of buildings can bring large savings compared to the cost of new buildings,[27] there were clear signs that the very process of conversion can increase community involvement. In a number of projects, conversion work was carried out by volunteer groups of young people. It gave them a physical involvement in the scheme which was important in creating a sense of personal achievement and in establishing a sound basis for future activities.[28]

Volunteers and professionals

145   The stress laid throughout this assessment on the potential of voluntary groups could by implication throw doubt on the role which professionals can play in the organisation of leisure. In point of fact, all the Leisure Experiments employed people in professional capacities, in addition to the small teams which worked to the Local Group. It is probably doubtful whether the Experiments could have been got off the ground effectively without the use of professionals. A distinction can be made in staffing between the small central teams which were set up (2 people in Sunderland and Stoke-on-Trent, 3 in Clwyd (Deeside), 4 in Dumbarton) and people employed to work on specific projects. In terms of full time equivalent posts over the period of the Experiments, Clwyd (Deeside) had 59¼ posts, Dumbarton 13½, Stoke-on-Trent 28½ and Sunderland 28¼. The substantially higher figure for Clwyd (Deeside) is accounted for by the 3 drama companies which were either set up or funded by the Experiment there. Professionals were used in one or more of 3 categories: as drama professionals; as teachers and specialists; and as community workers.

146   In addition to the professional workers there were large numbers of volunteers. Over 5,000 people were actively involved in helping to organise and run the projects supported by the 4 Experiments, most of them not merely supporting professionals but operating on their own. There are, of course, some practical difficulties and limitations to the involvement of volunteers. Most have work, education or domestic commitments and too much cannot be asked of them. Nevertheless the

27 The prime examples are the Burslem Leisure Centre in Stoke-on-Trent, project no.4 and the Central Information Office in Sunderland, project no.14. But the Gladstone Centre, project no.18, and the Islamic Cultural Centre, project no.21, both also in the Stoke-on-Trent Experiment, demonstrate the same point.
28 The Outdoor Activities Langdale project in Sunderland is an especially good example — project no. 26.

experience of the Experiments and the feelings of people involved point to the conclusion that full time organisers need only be used very sparingly. The main focus of professional work, as seen by voluntary bodies, is on strengthening the ability of groups to become self-supporting and on providing unobtrusive help.

147 In many of the projects in which professionals and volunteers worked side by side, relations were harmonious and constructive. This was particularly so where professionals had a 'traditional' role as teacher or demonstrator. There were some problems in cases where roles were not clearly defined. This seemed to be particularly the case where the management of schemes for children was concerned. However, there were only 1 or 2 schemes in all the Experiments in which the community proved unwilling to accept professionals. A lesson which the Experiments have driven home is how important it is to send professional community workers into the field with proper support. Flexibility, administrative back-up and access to the workings of local government and other agencies are needed if the workers are to establish credibility with members of the community.

The Leisure Experiments as action research

148 In paragraphs 1 to 9 the Leisure Experiments were placed in the context of a series of action research programmes which government has sponsored since the late 1960s. The way in which a research element was from the beginning built into the central and local structures of the Experiments was described in paragraphs 15 to 23.

149 Throughout the whole action period of the Experiments, and for a time afterwards, the Management Assessors and Project Evaluators whose work has been described in paragraphs 19 to 23 were working with and alongside the Local Groups and their officers, monitoring projects and developments and preparing the material which provides the basis for much of this Report.

150 A detailed discussion of the design and implementation of evaluation, prepared by the Central Research Co-ordinator forms Paper 2 in Volume 2. All action research programmes face a number of technical and management problems. The scheme of evaluation for the Experiments was intended to minimise these as far as possible in the light of previous experience and, to a very large extent, things worked out as intended. The understanding reached between Central and Local Sponsors on the place of research in the Experiments was never in doubt. The arrangements made for central co-ordination of evaluation worked smoothly.

151 In relation to the overall costs of the Experiments, the cost of evaluation was modest. Preliminary estimates had put the likely cost of local research at a little less than 10 per cent of the funds available to Local

Groups. In the event, final costs were nearer 5 per cent of local funds —
low by the standards of comparable exercises.

152   A particularly successful aspect of the Experiments was the degree
of harmony locally between the people who represented the Experiments'
commitment to action and those who represented the commitment to
research. Management Assessors carried off their task modestly and
capably and without forfeiting the trust of Local Groups. There was
evidence from all the Experiments that Project Evaluators personally
and the evaluation process in general helped action teams and individuals
concerned with projects to work more effectively.

153   The technical conduct of evaluation was very much affected by the
heavy work load carried by the Project Evaluators and by the equally heavy
burdens on action teams. This limited the degree of detail into which
individual evaluation exercises could go. But a further factor constrain-
ing detail was the decision to make evaluation as unobtrusive as possible.
Especially where voluntary groups were concerned it was necessary to
introduce evaluation by consent and to maintain a sense of proportion
in the balance between action and investigation. These constraints, partly
accepted voluntarily and partly inherent in the way the Experiments were
set up, meant that rigorously quantitative measures were not possible for
most projects, and the qualitative and quantitative aspects of the evaluation went hand in hand. Genuine rigour is, in any case, something rarely
achieved in the social sciences. Project Evaluators were in fact able to
collect a good deal of useful numerical information, which they were able
to use perceptively because of their close insight into the workings of the
Experiments.

154   The evaluation programme in the Experiments worked equally
effectively on an 'in-house' basis, where the Evaluator was recruited
directly to work with the action team; and on a 'consultancy' basis, where
the Evaluator was seconded from an academic institution. An independent but sympathetic presence in each Experiment, trained in observation
and analysis, proved invaluable to the Central Sponsors of the Experiments and helpful to the people directly involved in action — professional
staff and volunteer workers. The Experiments strongly confirmed the
value of including a social scientist in a programme of experimental
action, whether or not it is technically designated 'action research'.

Leisure and the quality of life:
the Experiments in retrospect

155   In paragraphs 95 to 154 we presented the lessons of the Experiments in the sequence in which they emerged. In this final section of our Report we look at them in terms of the original concept.

156   The Experiments were launched under the general banner of 'improving the quality of life' but there is no reliable way of assessing how much they contributed to the quality of life in the 4 areas. The very concept of 'quality of life' is a subject of lively controversy among academics[29] and there are no methods of measuring its various definitions sufficiently well established to have warranted the expense of special 'after' surveys for this Report. As earlier sections have indicated, however, the emphasis of the Experiments lay in providing the means by which people could improve their leisure life by their own efforts or in helping them to enrich the life of others. Several hundred thousand people were involved in 1 way or another in the Experiments and wide-ranging programmes of projects were undertaken. In all 4 areas the general level of leisure-time activities in voluntary groups, clubs and societies is — so far as can be judged — higher now than at the start of the Experiments. There is considerable evidence to support the general impression of enrichment.

157   A basic part of the original concept was to test the response to a locally-led campaign for community improvement. Here the results were beyond doubt. The Experiments provided clear confirmation of the potential for self-help and constructive involvement which exists in the community and the big and useful role of the voluntary organisations. The ideas underlying this aspect of the Experiments were not, of course, new nor was the response unexpected, but it was heartening to have such positive results. Leadership was found to be almost always a prerequisite of success for new or developing interests and the Groups sought by various means, not always successful, to encourage and identify community leaders. It was noteworthy that in Experiments dedicated to maximising recreational activities all the Groups exhibited a marked degree of concern for 'social service' objectives.[30] Apart from this, what was more surprising as well as particularly relevant in the cold economic climate of today, was the relatively modest means by which community potential could be released. Much of the practical evidence here came from the development of 3 out of the 4 Experiment headquarters as resource and information centres and the part played by the Experiment teams in helping voluntary organisations to 'work the system', directing them to the right source of help and generally acting as a connecting link between the statutory agencies and those wishing to make use of their services. Crucial also was the need for mutual understanding and sympathy between statutory providers and voluntary organisations and groups. We return to this later.

---

[29] See Paper 21 of Volume 2.
[30] In Dumbarton, however, sponsorship by the Youth and Community Service pointed the Experiment in this direction from the start.

158   The Groups were less successful in their attempts to draw on the full range of organisations and interests — also part of the local terms of reference — or to get through to local residents generally. Those who responded to the challenge of the Experiments were largely those who in 1 way or another were already committed to social or leisure pursuits. Putting in more professional organisers might have helped — this was a view expressed by some Local Group Chairmen and Directors at the close of the Experiment — though it must be also noted that where they were used, the results were highly variable. It is possible that had the Experiments run rather longer the 'second wave' of interest observed by the Evaluators (paragraph 129) might have gained in strength. As it is, the evidence remains inconclusive.

159   The original announcement spoke of bringing together 'a full range of leisure resources — cultural, recreational and sporting' and the local terms of reference amplified this in terms of 'ensuring the optimum use of existing leisure facilities and the addition of new...'. Of the many projects undertaken in the Experiments, few were new in themselves (though many were new to the Experiment areas) but much was done to develop and extend existing ideas and initiatives. One interesting feature which has relevance to the policies of local authorities was the imaginative use of buildings. The Experiments confirmed the undiminished importance of schools as potential community resources. Where community use had already been developed in purpose-built schools, much was already going on. But the Experiments showed that even older schools could be intensively used provided the practical details of staffing, opening hours, costing and cleaning could be coped with efficiently. Perhaps even more interestingly, the Experiments had several examples of what could be done with imagination, skill and a little money to old buildings which have only a limited life remaining. Many voluntary bodies preferred adapted or converted premises — shops, warehouses and town halls — to what they sometimes saw as the institutional character of local authority buildings. Costs were very much lower than those of new buildings, emphasising an important lesson of the Experiments — that useful changes in policy can be carried through without extra calls on costs and manpower provided reallocation of resources is planned in good time and with goodwill.

160   One of the main hopes of the Experiments, heavily supported as they were by funds channelled through national and regional arts organisations, was that they would throw light on what forms of art local communities most appreciate and in particular whether there are existing or potential requirements so far unmet. Clearly, limited experiments in 4 localities only could not be expected to provide definitive answers to the many questions implicit in this, but a number of pointers emerged. These are to be found in the data from the initial surveys (which might well repay closer investigation), in the accounts of local meetings and discussions, and more positively in the response of communities to new opportunities opened to them. There were also encouraging signs from projects continuing when the action periods ended that a number of such activities are wanted sufficiently to survive despite the present need for economies. It is evident, however, that much still remains to be discovered about the

wishes of local communities and that changes in people's patterns of leisure activities and preferences can be a slow business.

161   In terms of numbers of people involved, well established types of artistic entertainment and effort were most successful and there did not seem, for example, to be any particular demand for innovatory art forms. This was not to say that demand could not be created. It was successfully done in a number of cases, especially where local colour could be invoked. None the less, a great deal of hard work was involved and the experiment with non-traditional cultural activities proved expensive in terms of the funds available to Local Groups without any guarantee of long term success. Traditional forms of entertainment met with more success, but 1 of the difficult questions which still has to be weighed in the light of the evidence is how far the relatively costly presentation of the arts by professional performers in new areas can be justified as against the obviously popular, and on the whole cheaper, provision of facilities for use by voluntary societies on their own initiatives seeking their professional help in their own way.

162   In general, opportunities for individual and group work in the arts met an enthusiastic response. Pottery, painting, jewellery, sculpting, photography and other regular 'evening class' favourites demonstrated continuing strength and vitality. Music-making especially in outlying communities was popular. In the arts as in other fields, the concept of the loan pool was particularly successful, whether as an extension of local authority activities as in a Picture Lending Library, or an Experiment-run equipment pool of filming equipment, musical instruments, sheet music, stage lighting and public address systems. The rising cost of equipment for amateur artists and sportsmen may make loan and pool services something which regional arts and sports bodies may increasingly wish to support in conjunction with local authorities.

163   The Experiments found that in all 4 areas local sports organisations and clubs were well established and doing well. There was scope for further action by regional sports bodies but that lay mainly in fields already referred to — support services for sports clubs, help with equipment often on a pooled basis; some pump-priming assistance to help new clubs to get through the first crucial season, and help in finding storage space for sports equipment. A big potential demand for camping and other outdoor activities developed among young people and on a family basis, particularly in the Sunderland and Dumbarton areas, and some particularly interesting and successful projects were mounted in response.

164   For both regional arts and sports agencies, the Experiments showed the importance of overcoming the impression of remoteness which they sometimes convey. Obviously, large regions and small staff mean that resources are stretched, but there is clearly a need for arrangements which can rapidly put local people in touch with the person who can best help them.

165   On the question of the geographical distribution of opportunity the experience of the Experiments seems to confirm that people are not

willing to travel very far for 'everyday' leisure activities. Most of the projects sponsored by the Experiments drew participants from the immediate area or the area close to the homes of the principal enthusiasts. Many local 'community' projects were very successful. This suggests that a localised network of leisure buildings and equipment might well suit most people's needs and wishes. Children, teenagers and old people in particular depend on public transport and the vagaries of route structure, fares and weather will closely affect the scope they have for pursuing independent leisure activities. Localised opportunities would thus appear to be an important element in sharing out opportunity. Of course, this does not affect the need for well sited specialist facilities to serve as major centres of excellence and the Experiment showed — for example in dry ski-ing and sky diving — that enthusiasts are willing to travel long distances to pursue their specialised activities.

166   As we have already suggested, 1 of the most telling lessons of the Experiments was the relatively small means needed to release local initiative and encourage voluntary activities. However, although the Experiments showed that striking results could be achieved by relatively modest support for voluntary organisations, the fact remains that the 4 Local Groups had substantial funds to draw on. The question may fairly be asked whether local authorities and others could hope to achieve comparable results without similar injections of fertisilising grants.

167   We believe the answer to be that they could. The funds contributed from central and local sources to make the Experiments possible were intended to act as a catalyst, demonstrating what could be achieved by local effort. Local authorities, other statutory agencies and some voluntary organisations, however, already have the bases on which to build, whereas the Local Groups had to develop them. Once organisations had been established locally, the effect of the funds at the Groups' disposal was largely to speed-up, intensify and extend the development of ideas and activities which were already in existence in one form or another.[31] Financial support was always a help but the amounts involved were often surprisingly small and loans and guarantees against loss often proved more valuable than cash handouts. Low-cost conversions and funding voluntary groups were shown to cost relatively very little compared for instance with the scale of local government expenditure on the construction, maintenance and servicing of many capital projects in the leisure field or with local authorities' annual revenue expenditure on recreation services. Sums of the order involved could be found by a very small reallocation of internal budgets. On the experience of the Experiments the benefits would be high.

168   Moreover, the Experiments showed that success was often as much a matter of relationships and sensible practical help as of money. Project reports indicated that a great deal of local initiative could be encouraged by making life easier for voluntary bodies in a variety of small ways which

---

[31] For example, the Community Theatre Project at Stoke-on-Trent, (project no. 12) where the Victoria Theatre was able to put into effect in a year's intensive effort ideas with which the Theatre Director had already begun to experiment.

are a matter of practical planning and goodwill rather than money. Examples — trivial in themselves but adding up to a considerable burden for inexperienced voluntary groups hoping to launch a new initiative — could include helping volunteers with problems of office administration, insurance, licensing, garaging and vehicle maintenance.

169   In paragraph 157 we have already touched on the importance of a relationship of mutual trust and confidence between statutory providers and volunteers. The Experiments showed the value of greater tolerance and understanding on both sides. Local authorities and other statutory agencies could show greater flexibility and informality — departmentalism can result in community initiatives becoming frustrated and their sponsors cynical. Equally, greater efforts could be made by people in the voluntary sector to understand the ways in whcih statutory bodies have to operate and to appreciate the real difficulties they face, especially in the current cutback of public expenditure.

170   It is, of course, easy to talk glibly about sympathy and understanding. Busy people in public offices with a heavy schedule of routine duties to get through often have real practical difficulties in making time to cope with volunteers, even where they have the will to do so. The experience of the Experiments suggests that if these difficulties are to be overcome there needs to be a conscious recognition of the gain to the community from harnessing voluntary effort and active steps need to be taken to plan for it. Mention has already been made of the value of resource and information centres. One of the lessons of the Experiments was that these could be provided in a variety of ways, not necessarily directly by local authorities, though they would benefit from local authority support. Much could be done as already suggested in making council owned premises more access- ible, treating the staff of leisure and recreation departments as a resource for the community, cutting red tape to the minimum where small grants are involved and dealing with imagination and sympathy with applications from those unfamiliar with official procedures. Local authorities contain a wealth of skills and imagination which deployed constructively for voluntary bodies could produce big results at relatively low cost.

171   As the opening section of the Report implied, the effectiveness of the Experiments will not be judged narrowly by their impact in Alyn and Deeside, Delyn, Dumbarton, Stoke-on-Trent and Sunderland, nor even on the influence they have on leisure policies. The Experiments will have justified the hopes vested in them if we absorb the more general lessons they have delivered — to draw local people more closely into things which affect them personally, to regard statutory agencies as resources to be used by people rather than impersonal, and apparently irrelevant, machines; and to make the best use of the reserves of resourcefulness, vitality, compassion and enthusiasm with which almost all communities are endowed — and by which the quality of life is ultimately measured.

Annex 1 (to Part 1)
Records of the Experiment

Project Records

For those wishing to study the Experiments more closely, arrangements have been made for evaluation and other local reports to be deposited as follows:

For all 4 Experiments

The Library[1]
Department of the Environment
2 Marsham Street
LONDON SW1P 3EB

For individual Experiments

Sunderland
The Library[1]
Sunderland Polytechnic
Chester Road
Sunderland SR1 3SD

Clwyd (Deeside)
Clwyd County Council[1]
Archives Department
Shire Hall
Mold
Clwyd CH7 6NB

Stoke-on-Trent
The Library[1]
North Staffordshire Polytechnic
College Road
Stoke-on-Trent ST4 2DE

Dumbarton
Andersonian Library[1]
University of Strathclyde
McCance Building
Richmond Street
Glasgow G11 XQ

Film of the Experiments

A film has been made showing some of the activities undertaken during the Experiments and is available for loan from the Central Film Library, Government Building, Bromyard Avenue, Acton, London W3.

[1] Prior notice should be given to the Chief Librarian.

Annex 2 (to Part 1)
Contributions to the Experiments

	£
Stoke-on-Trent	
Stoke-on-Trent City Council	40,000
Staffordshire County Council	5,000
Department of Education & Science (through West Midlands Arts)	100,000
Department of the Environment	100,000
	245,000
Sunderland	
Sunderland Metropolitan Borough Council	40,000
Tyne & Wear Metropolitan County Council	40,000
Department of Education & Science (through Northern Arts)	100,000
Department of the Environment	100,000
	280,000
Clwyd (Deeside)	
Clwyd County Council	50,000
Delyn Borough Council	25,000
Alyn & Deeside District Council	25,000
Department of Education & Science (through Welsh Arts Council)	100,000
Welsh Office	11,000
Welsh Sports Council	10,000
Department of Education & Science (for research)	10,000
Department of the Environment (for research)	20,000
	251,000
Dumbarton[1]	
Former Dumbarton Burgh Council	18,600
Former Helensburgh Burgh Council	3,500
Former Helensburgh District Council	3,500
Former Vale of Leven District Council	8,600
Former Dunbartonshire Education Committee	8,600
Strathclyde Regional Council Education Committee	8,200
Department of Education and Science (through Scottish Arts Council)	100,000
Scottish Education Department	70,000
Scottish Sports Council	30,000
Department of the Environment (for research)	10,000
	251,000

[1] The figures are based on the final local report to the Local Group in November 1976 pending a final financial statement.

53

1   Sunderland project no 2
Listening to the Band in a Sunderland Park

2   Stoke-on-Trent
project no 24
The first 'Do It
Yourself' Messiah in
Hanley

4   Clwyd (Deeside)
project no 105
A Poetry Circle is
formed
By kind permission
Clwyd County
Council

Left
6   Clwyd (Deeside)
project no 123
Hawkesbury Visual
Arts Centre, Buckley
*By kind permission
of Clwyd County
Council*

Above
5   Dumbarton
project no 162
Audience reaction
to a video tape of
themselves by
themselves in
Ladyton
*Photograph by
David Mitchell*

Above
7   Sunderland project no 43 Wearabout Theatre Company helped by primary school children perform 'Ulysses'.
Nothern Echo photograph

Right
8   Dumbarton project no 73 Cycles on loan from Garelochead Outdoor Centre
Photograph by David Mitchell

Below
9   Stoke-on-
Trent project no 28
Play for Children
where no play
facilities exist

At foot
10   Dumbarton
project no 107
Taking part in a
Movement Festival
Display
*Photograph by
David Mitchell*

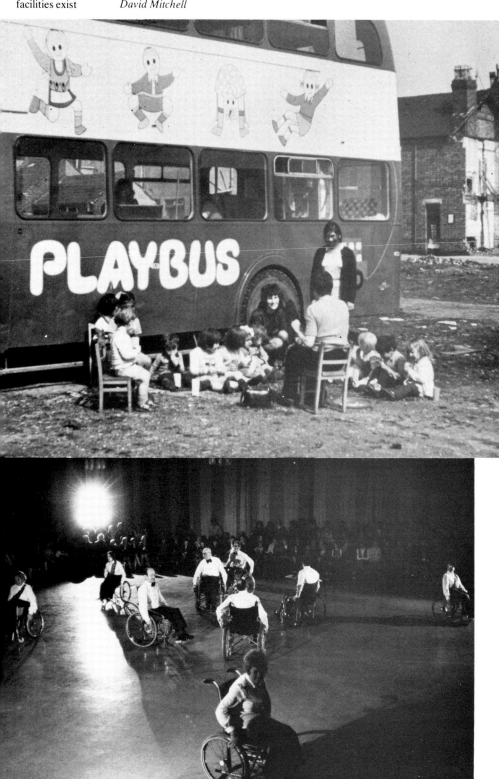

11   Dumbarton
project no 4
Rush to greet the
Arts Bus on
Alexandria Gala
Day, Vale of Leven.
Photograph by
David Mitchell

12   Clwyd (Deeside)
project no 102
A new amateur
orchestra is started
By kind permission of
Clwyd County Council

14   Sunderland
project no 26
Busy on conversion
at Langdale Outdoor
Education Centre

13   Dumbarton
project no 78
Walkers climbing
Carman Hill, near
Renton, Vale of
Leven on the first
Guided Walk
*Photograph by
David Mitchell*

Left and below
15, 16   Stoke-on-
Trent project no 18
Members of the
Saturday Club try
their hand and
exhibit their wares
in the Gladstone
Centre
*By kind permission
of the Gladstone
Pottery Museum*

Part 2

The Experiments in action

The Experiments in action
Introduction

1   This part of our Report consists of an account of the 4 local Experiments in chronological order, beginning with Sunderland, where the Local Group held their first meeting on 28 November 1973 and disbanded on 24 March 1976, and ending with Dumbarton where the action period ran until 31 August 1976, and reporting continued to November.

2   The accounts which follow have been compiled centrally from the reports, papers and minutes of the Local Groups themselves, the confidential reports of the Management Assessors and the reports of Evaluators. Although, as explained in Part 1, the Experiments were undertaken in a common framework, records and reports naturally varied in extent, style and content just as the Local Groups themselves varied in structure, methods and make-up of their action programmes. Drawing on the extensive material available, we have not attempted to force the 4 accounts into a standard pattern but to give a clear and reasonably concise account of each Experiment, conveying as much of the local flavour as is possible when writing at one remove. Each account is backed by a summary catalogue of the projects undertaken but a fuller picture of the wide range of activities and the degree of success they achieved can be obtained by consulting the detailed project catalogue at Paper 3 of Volume 2.

3   Throughout Part 1 of the Report we referred for convenience to the 'Local Groups' running the Experiments. In fact, each Local Group adopted its own name and style. These, with particulars of members, staff, etc., are given at the start of each account and each Group is referred to thereafter by the name by which it is known locally.

4   The costs of individual projects are given in the catalogues which follow each account. All the Experiments had minor differences in their accounting methods but for the purpose of this report we have, so far as possible, sought to standardise costing. In all cases therefore only costs to the Experiment are given, although for projects where money is known to have been made available from other agencies towards the overall cost, this is indicated by an asterisk. The cost quoted includes the initial costs of, for example, various transport vehicles, pools of equipment, etc., which will remain in the Experiment areas.

5   Funds allocated at the start of each Experiment were inevitably eroded by inflation during the period of action. Local Groups were asked to keep within the original allocations and they all co-operated by adjusting their programmes where necessary. It is perhaps appropriate here to express again appreciation of the work of those who undertook the big responsibility, financial and otherwise, involved in running the Experiments locally, and of the many who contributed enthusiasm, energy and dedication to carrying through the project programmes.

The Sunderland Experiment

locally known as
The Experiment in Leisure Project (E L P)

Local Sponsors
Sunderland Metropolitan Borough Council
Tyne & Wear Metropolitan County Council
Northern Arts
Northern Sports Council

Experiment Area
Before Local Government Reorganisation
Sunderland County Borough, Hetton, Houghton-le-Spring, Washington
Urban Districts of County Durham

After Local Government Reorganisation
Sunderland Metropolitan Borough of Tyne & Wear Metropolitan County

Population
294,000 (December 1973)

Experiment Headquarters
27 Stockton Road, Sunderland

Local organisation

Local Sponsors Group
(outline policy and selection of Project Team).

Members

Cllr L Harper (Chairman)
Sunderland Metropolitan Borough
Council

J Tatchell
Chairman of Northern Arts — initial
meetings

Cllr S V Heatlie
Tyne & Wear Metropolitan County
Council, Chairman of Northern Arts —
later meetings

J S Calvert
Chairman of Northern Sports Council

Project Team
(executive function and control of Experiment programme)

Members

D A Sanford (Leader)

Cllr R C Baxter
Sunderland Metropolitan Borough Council

Cllr F Ipey
Tyne & Wear Metropolitan County Council

Mrs M E Garrood
Northern Arts (to October 1975)

I Clarke
Northern Arts (from November 1975)

W Saunders
Northern Sports Council

R Chapman
Department of the Environment Northern
Region

Mrs B Cohen
Also Assessor for the Experiment

Miss S Cook (February to June 1974)

T Forster

D Gibson

Miss F Hetherington
(February to June 1974)

C B Jones

P Latham (From January 1975)

J O'Toole (to June 1974)

P Stewart

K Stitt (to January 1975)

Rev K Stock

K Witherington

Project Team Sub-Groups

C B Jones (Chairman: *Music*)
(to January 1975)

P Latham (Chairman: *Music*)
(from January 1975)

K Howard (Chairman: *Outdoor Activities*)

Rev K stock (Chairman: *Transport Pool*)

J R Kayll (Chairman: *Water Activities*)

Experiment Team

R Birks Coordinator

P Thompson Administrator

Evaluator

C J Horn

Map 1.
Sunderland Experiment Area

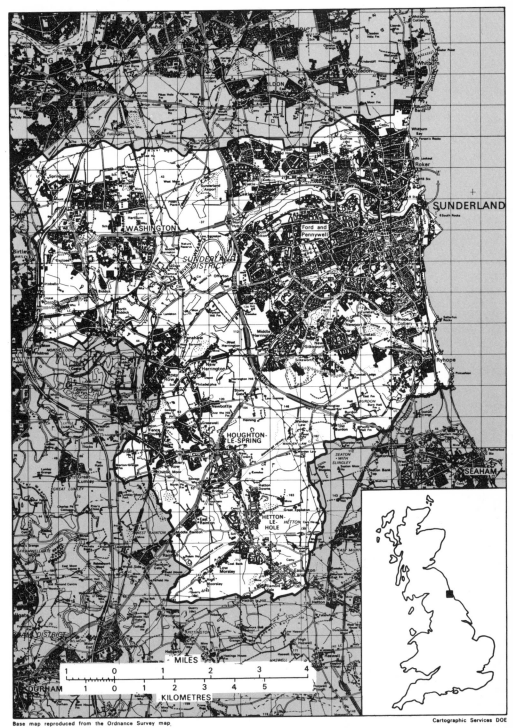

Base map reproduced from the Ordnance Survey map.

Cartographic Services DOE

The Sunderland Experiment

1   Sunderland is a town of contrasts. Standing at the mouth of the River Wear and looking to Wearside rather than the Tyneside complex, it is both seaport and seaside resort. To its long history of coalmining and shipbuilding it has in more recent years added a wide variety of other industries and commercial occupations, as well as being a centre for services, recreation and shopping in north east Durham. To the west is the rapidly developing new town of Washington, started in 1964 and as with all the new towns planning ahead for the social and leisure needs of its 'new' population. To the south of the Wear and half way between Sunderland and Durham are the other 2 urban centres of the Experiment area, the mining towns of Hetton and Houghton-le-Spring. Coalmining, formerly active over a much wider area, has left a pattern of mining communities in which the Workingmen's Clubs remain a feature — indeed for some, almost a way of life. In the year the Experiment was launched, Sunderland was celebrating its football team's victory in the Cup Final and in the 'Wearmouth 1300 Festival' the anniversary of the birth of the Venerable Bede and of the founding of the famous Monkwearmouth Monastery, where he spent his early years. Appropriately enough, in 1973, too, a new arts centre was opened and a large sports complex was in the planning stages.

Setting up the Experiment

2   The Sunderland Experiment was sponsored locally by a group comprising representatives of the new Metropolitan Borough of Sunderland, Tyne and Wear Metropolitan County Council, Northern Arts and the Northern Sports Council, with Sunderland in the chair. These sponsors initiated the Experiment, selected the Local Group who were to be responsible for policy, allocation of funds, general management and evaluation of projects, and recommended broad guidelines for the Experiment. They did not play a direct part thereafter though they continued to keep in touch with progress. To form the Local Group they chose 12 members combining representatives of the 4 Local Sponsors with others selected individually for their experience and lively interest in leisure pursuits. The Group was led by Denis Sanford, a surgeon well known locally for his contribution to cultural and social work in Sunderland. To stress the 'action' character of the Experiment the Group decided to call itself the Project Team[1] with Denis Sanford as Team Leader, and the Experiment became known locally as the 'Experiment in Leisure Project' or ELP for short.

3   The Project Team were helped to get off to a quick start by having from

---

[1] In the other 3 Experiments the officers were known as the 'Project Team' or 'Team'. In Part 1 where the 4 Experiments are referred to collectively and individually the term 'Local Group' is used for the Sunderland Project Team and 'Team' for the Sunderland officers.

the beginning the services of an Administrator, transferred from Sunderland MBC. They appointed a Co-ordinator and Evaluator early in the following year with 2 clerical assistants in support. All the staff remained with the Experiment throughout the action period and were fully committed to its aims. Other staff were taken on as needed for individual projects. Meeting fortnightly, with the Co-ordinator, Administrator and Evaluator taking a full part in discussion, members and staff developed a strong team spirit and exercised close control throughout.

4 The funds available for the Experiment totalled £280,000, Sunderland Borough Council and Tyne and Wear County Council contributing £40,000 each in addition to the Central Sponsors' contributions. With the Project Team controlling the allocation, the finances were handled through the Sunderland Treasurer.

Programme approach

5 From the beginning, the Project Team adopted a 'learn-as-you-go' approach. This accorded with the guidelines recommended by the Local Sponsors who were concerned that the first momentum of the Experiments should not be lost. It was influenced also by some initial uncertainty about the dates within which the 2-year action period was to run. As a result the programme fell into 2 parts, the first year concentrating on action and the second giving priority to evaluation while using the remaining funds for selected projects which experience suggested might be most rewarding. Other guidelines given by the Sponsors were that there should not be too many projects; that projects should be new to Sunderland although not necessarily new in concept, and should be capable of evaluation; that the Experiment should not take the form of a festival; and that a measure of success would be the extent to which activities were ongoing at the conclusion of the Experiment. These recommendations were developed by the Project Team into a number of general objectives and criteria against which every proposed project was subsequently considered. Prominent among their aims was to show the individual, by example, the opportunities available for developing a capacity for choice during his/her leisure time and to consider whether existing processes gave groups sufficient choice of opportunity. Proposals were examined to see whether among other things they would develop leadership, were likely to continue without support from the Experiment or other organisation, or would bring together different age groups to work together. Where an idea seemed worth adopting, the Project Team and staff made every effort to develop it into a suitable project even though it met the criteria only marginally when first proposed.

Handling the projects

6 Once the Project Team got under way it quickly became clear to them that they could not expect to consider every idea exhaustively in the form in which it was initially received. To deal with this they set up a series of

sub-groups which drew more voluntary interests, both individuals and organisations, into the Experiment. The choice of sub-groups was based partly on the collective experience and views of Project Team members, partly on the ideas received in response to initial publicity. The sub-groups covered Outdoor Activities, Music, Drama, Transport and Water Activities. In each, a member of the Project Team undertook to provide a direct link with the Team, acting as chairman in most cases. The Water Activities Sub-Group elected an independent chairman and this Sub-Group very soon formed itself into an association of all water users of the River Wear, becoming self supporting and virtually independent of the Experiment.

7   The earlier projects were discussed at length by the full Team, but a method of handling ideas was soon evolved which worked easily and saved time. Each idea was first discussed with the proposer, who was then helped to prepare an outline proposal on a form specially designed for the purpose. This was discussed by the Project Team and proposals of merit were referred back to sub-groups and officers for preparation of a detailed worksheet which covered arrangements for organisation, management, financing and an outline of the evaluation to be carried out. The worksheet was then submitted to the Project Team for decision and if accepted formed a contract for the project. The hallmark of this method was close co-operation at critical stages between project proposers, Experiment officials, sub-groups and members of the Project Team. It also made it easy for evaluation to be an integral part of the planning and development of each project.

Identifying needs

8   The Project Team tried in a number of ways to discover what needs existed in Sunderland. They considered commissioning a market research survey but decided against this method. Instead they tried out various ways of encouraging members of organisations or of the general public to come forward with their own ideas. One of the first actions of the Project Team was to circulate letters to approximately 1,000 known organisations asking for suggestions — 140 were received, including some, which as already mentioned, materially influenced the choice of major projects. Individual members of the Project Team volunteered to follow up these ideas and the outcome was the formation of the sub-groups. Throughout the Experiment news reports were given to local press and radio with a view to generating interest. Talks were given on local radio and television stations. Prepaid suggestion post cards were sent to commercial addresses. 'Ideas leaflets' were widely distributed. Later in the Experiment efforts were made to check if gaps still remained and the Project Team decided to investigate the position in depth in a selected part of Sunderland. A survey was commissioned covering the Pennywell, Ford and South Hylton areas. This was a project in itself and the outcome was agreement to support the provision of an adventure playground. Other needs emerged in discussing project proposals — for example many organisations were found to have

inadequate space for their activities and the Team instituted a search for premises which might be adapted for leisure use.

The projects

9   Altogether the Team considered 165 ideas and from these developed and financed 40 major projects. Projects were normally funded for a 12-month period. Some carried out in the first part of the Experiment were in fact taken over by other organisations in the second year. Sunderland Borough Council, in particular, took on a number of schemes begun by the Experiment — 2 of these were the Neighbourhood Playschemes referred to later in paragraph 15 and the Bands in Parks project which in the Experiment took the form of a series of concerts of varying kinds of music — brass and jazz, folk and pop — in different parks.

10   The idea of establishing an Experiment Headquarters separate from the main Civic Centre had been raised at the original meeting of Local Sponsors. The Project Team first considered adapting a Victorian pub to use as a study headquarters and develop as a meeting and information centre. This scheme had to be abandoned because of problems over planning and fire regulations and after a district wide scour for premises an old bakery was eventually converted into a colourful and lively information centre easily accessible from the main shopping areas of the town. This developed into a general resource centre and by the second year of the Experiment it had become an accepted source of information and advice, a headquarters for a number of projects, a store for equipment and a place to come to and discuss ideas. The centre served as a meeting place for voluntary organisations and the staff were often able to provide a bridge between local authority services and voluntary bodies informing people where help might be obtained and discussing with local authority departments when needs were discovered and/or suggestions made. Groups of like interests were put in touch with each other. The Experiment staff also developed a supportive role for many local community activities. Helping with the organisation of Workingmen's Clubs' fetes and other events and a charity marathon swim are examples of the many ways in which their resources were used, and in carrying through such commitments they were able to help the community to discover its own needs. To develop the information service still further a specially constructed Mobile Information Vehicle was acquired to serve also as a ticket booking agency. It was run as an integral part of the Information Centre set up in the headquarters with staff taken on specially for the purpose. Equipped with loud speakers the vehicle also contributed to local events and helped provide publicity for them.

11   The Team experimented with Community Drama. Initially discussions were held with a local Live Theatre Company. A number of performances in schools were given but the Project Team were reluctantly compelled to abandon the scheme because the Company were unwilling to work within the conditions of the Experiment, wanting to operate quite independently. Instead the Project Team set up a professional theatre

group under the supervision of its Drama Sub-Group and with a professional director. The Wearabout Theatre Company, as it became known, gave a number of different productions to different kinds of audiences and was particularly successful with its productions in schools. As a result, Sunderland agreed to give support to the project in the second year when a Management Committee was formed to run the Company.

12   Early suggestions received by the Project Team highlighted 2 particular areas of need. The first was for some form of transport to provide the chance to take part in leisure activities to a wide range of people who were ordinarily unable to do so. The second was for a variety of items of equipment the provision of which was beyond the scope of informal groups and organisations. The Project Team therefore developed a range of major projects which were serviced by a transport pool. This started with 2 mini buses coming into operation from May 1974 and which were used to take people to places and activities of their choice. The Wearabout Theatre Company had the use of a van; a specially adapted vehicle — Dial-a-Bus — was provided for use by the handicapped and a Nature Bus was designed and equipped as a travelling biology classroom to take children on study trips into the country.

13   Various equipment pools were also provided. A number of musical instruments were puchased and lodged at 3 schools in the district where weekly classes were arranged. A comprehensive school at Ryhope became the caretakers of a pool of stage lighting and audio equipment, maintained and run under supervision by the pupils themselves. A large store of equipment for outdoor activities was organised and managed by a co-ordinator taken on for the purpose. Developing the loan system for some 1,200 items of equipment was not his only task; additionally he became a useful source of information and stimulated interest in outdoor activities generally.

14   The Central Outdoor Activities Equipment Pool was used, as was the Transport Pool, in conjunction with 3 Outdoor Activity Centres where children and young people could go for climbing, hill walking and other outdoor pursuits. Two of these centres — the Ewart Centre in Northumberland and Middleton Camp in Teesdale — were already in existence but were helped to develop and expand. In the third, the Langdale Centre in the Lakes, an old building was converted by a group of young people who did all the work themselves under the guidance of a Sunderland schoolteacher. It was extensively used during the Experiment and is being continued by a Management Committee made up of representatives of those using the Centre and of the Sunderland community.

15   In many of their schemes the Project Team sought to encourage individuals and groups to develop latent potential for managing activities as well as taking part in them. A distinguishing feature of their support for Neighbourhood Playschemes was that they were schemes based on local initiative. They were managed by local groups — parents, teachers and volunteers — and with the support of a full time co-ordinator the groups evolved a system of regular meetings to discuss and deal with

common problems. Similarly, in the case of a project for the multi-use of premises in 3 local schools (started with the support of the Sunderland Education and Leisure Committees) it was left to each local organising group to adapt the general structure of the project to the needs and demands of their own community. The practical problems of using schools for community leisure activities out of hours were ovecome by appointing 2 teachers at each school to co-ordinate the after hours use. At each school a School Users Committee took responsibility for the evening activities and these committees are continuing with support from the Sunderland Education Committee.

16   An attempt to involve young people in the Experiment began with a 1-day Schools Conference which sought to awaken interest in older pupils and identify some who might take the lead in future activities. This was followed by the setting up of a Youth Leisure Group comprised entirely of young members who were encouraged to operate as a junior Project Team, taking full responsibility for the projects they sponsored. Some of these projects were successful and were likely to continue. The Youth Leisure Group itself did not survive the Experiment, however, since the original members became involved in other interests and no successors emerged to take over from them.

17   Altogether the project programme covered a wide range of interests including theatre, music, community arts, sports, indoor and outdoor activities, as well as activities specially designed for children, young people and senior citizens. Projects took place for the most part within the newly constituted Sunderland Metropolitan Borough, in Washington, Hetton and Houghton as well as in the main urban concentration of Sunderland itself. This involved the Project Team in co-operation with communities which had previously had independent administrations and with Washington New Town Corporation. One example of the latter was the 'Insticart' project, which involved development of a temporary arts centre in a former miners' institute in Washington. Its purpose was to help the Arts Organiser for Washington to experiment in a range of arts activities some of which were later transferred to the new and permanent arts centre at Biddick Farm. A few of the more important projects extended beyond the borough boundaries. Subscription concerts and the International Folk Moot drew audiences from far afield and the Mobile Information Vehicle — a purpose built information centre run by 2 full-time staff — travelled within the catchment area of the Empire Theatre.

18   The projects varied in complexity and organisation. Some which were organised on a voluntary basis by individuals (Amateur Academics) or organisations (the Scouts' Camping and Open Country for the Family project) cost relatively little. More complex projects were organised by people who were employed specifically for this purpose. Examples include the Director of the Mobile Theatre Company (Wearabout) and the Co-ordinator who managed the Outdoor Activity projects and ran the Central Pool of Equipment. Not all complex projects were necessarily costly. Underwriting by the Project Team and the provision of petty cash helped in many instances. Most projects benefited from a good deal of

volunteer effort and assistance; all of them added to the resources put in by the Experiment by fund-raising and other efforts.

19   An important feature of the Sunderland Experiment was the value which the Project Team attached to the process of evaluation. The Evaluator was regarded as a resource not only for the Central Sponsors of the Experiment but also for the local Team. Close attention to the spirit of evaluation meant that proposers and the Project Team combined to identify objectives and that projects were carefully prepared and structured. Moreover, feedback of evaluation reports during the action period helped the Team to improve the quality of the decisions which it made on future action.

Ongoing arrangements

20   Although action had mainly finished by the end of 1975, ongoing arrangements and writing up continued into 1976. The Project Team was disbanded in March 1976. They had striven in their last year to find some way in which the service and goodwill built up from the Experiment Centre could be continued but were not able to achieve this to their entire satisfaction and as a result did not complete the full conversion of the premises as a central store which they had earlier planned. Nevertheless, arrangements were made for the Centre to be used by the Sunderland Arts Centre with agreement that organisations and groups in the habit of using it for meetings could continue to do so. During the winding up stages, Tyne and Wear County Council had suggested that the Outdoor Activities equipment might be made available to serve a wider area but in the event it was decided that it should be retained in Sunderland and moved from the Experiment Centre to other premises with support from the Borough Council. It was to be run by a form of management trust — a Borough Outdoor Activities Association consisting of representatives of the Borough and of voluntary organisations. Management Trusts on similar lines were also set up to run 2 out of 3 of the outdoor centres and the Wearabout Theatre Company, was also continued by a Management Trust under the umbrella of Sunderland Arts Centre Management Committee. Reference has already been made to a number of other projects which were to continue with local authority support, e.g. the multi use of school premises. Sunderland's Recreation Department also took over the information function of the Experiment Centre but moved it to operate from the departmental offices in Houghton-le-Spring. In summary, of the 40 major projects undertaken 31 were continuing and being developed; most others were continuing on a reduced scale. Very few projects had ceased completely.

Sunderland Experiment

Summary of projects *(for fuller details see Paper 3 in Volume 2)*

Ref. No.	Name of Project	Summary Description	Cost to Experiment £
1	**Amateur Academics**	Family day-trips with qualified leaders to places of academic interest.	406
2-3	**Bands in Parks**		4,239
2	*Band Concerts*	Programme of 8 Sunday band concerts arranged in 3 local parks during summer 1974.	
3	*Contemporary Folk Concerts*	Programme of Contemporary Folk Concerts.	
4	**Board Games Centre**	Board Games evenings at Experiment Centre — held 3 nights, weekly.	137
5	**Camping and the Open Country for the Family**	Exhibitions and demonstrations on camping to give guidance to people.	1,900
6	**Coelfrith Early Music Society**	Concerts and work shops to encourage interest in early music. Experiment underwrote costs of existing society.	1,100*
7	**Charity Marathon – Swim '75**	Sponsored swim for fun and to raise money for charity.	500
8	**Community Arts Officer**	Officer appointed to help Sunderland Arts Centre develop a programme of community arts.	2,133
9	**Experiment Centre, Stockton Road Sunderland**	Conversion of old bakery into an Experiment Centre and a Study Headquarters.	14,141
10-11	**Film Making**		741
10	*Community Film Club*	Projector provided for local film club to enable it to present films to different groups.	
11	*Film Making*	Equipment to encourage young people under qualified leadership to make films as a means of expressing ideas.	
12	**Five Quarter Rapper Team**	Equipment for dance team to encourage traditional dancing and plays.	52
13	**Greater use of Workingmen's Clubs**	Old people's club formed in a Working-men's Club.	360

Ref. No.	Name of Project	Summary Description	Cost to Experiment £
14-15	**Information Service**		
14	*Central Information Office*	Office providing comprehensive information service on leisure activities, housed in Experiment Centre.	4,827
15	*Mobile Information Vehicle*	Mobile ticket-booking and information office.	8,432*
16	**International Youth Festival of Folk Dance and Music**	Help to extend Festival for Youth in 1975.	4,000*
17	**Leisure Transport Pool**	Self-drive Mini Buses made available for group booking.	4,105
18	**Leisure Transport for the Severely Handicapped**	Purpose-built ambulance to transport severely handicapped of all ages and to give them the chance to go out.	6,104
19	**Multi-use of Local Authority Premises**	Extended use of schools for people of all ages in 3 parts of the Borough. Evening Principals appointed and User Committees established.	2,496
20	**Musical Instruments Pool**	Equipment to encourage younger teenagers in classical music — instruments and sheet music available for loan.	5,003
21	**Nature Bus**	Travelling biology classroom in converted bus for children in inner urban areas.	4,833
22	**Neighbourhood Playschemes**	16 Playschemes run by volunteer groups.	12,224
23	**Olympic Gymnastics for Girls**	Weekly classes with qualified coach at local school.	439
24-27	**Outdoor Activities**		
24	*Co-ordinator and Central Pool of Equipment*	Co-ordinator appointed and Central Pool of outdoor equipment provided — operating from the Experiment Centre.	24,188
25	*Ewart Centre*	Financial help to YMCA volunteers to develop an outdoor activities centre in Northumberland.	8,485*
26	*Langdale Outdoor Education Centre*	Financial help to young volunteers to develop an outdoor activities centre in the Lake District.	12,156

Ref. No.	Name of Project	Summary Description	Cost to Experiment £
27	*Middleton Camp*	Financial help to upgrade existing Sunderland schools' camp in Teesdale.	9,585
28	**Roller Skating in Barnes Park**	80 morning and afternoon children's skating sessions as an extension of Sunderland Borough Council's play leadership schemes.	2,882
29	**Ryhope Stage Lighting and Audio Equipment Pool**	Theatrical equipment for a local school to serve a wide range of amateur groups.	2,830
30-35	**Small Projects**	Various small projects sponsored by the Experiment including Live Theatre, a Schools Conference.	3,750
36	**Soundwaves**	Equipment and funds for news tapes for the blind or partially sighted, produced in the form of a monthly magazine.	219
37	**Stannington School Leisure Centre**	Support for a scheme to open an ESN school as a leisure centre for children and parents.	818
38	**Subscription Concerts**	Quality concerts at the Empire Theatre to demonstrate that there is an audience for classical music.	2,728*
39	**Sunderland Playbus (Extension)**	Extended use of existing playbus.	6,917
40-41	**Survey of a Selected Neighbourhood Area**		
40	*Survey*	Survey in certain areas with limited leisure amenities. Intended to be complementary to a recent survey by Sunderland Borough Council.	3,449
41	*Adventure Playground Project (Pennywell)*	Contribution towards an Adventure Playground to meet need identified by survey.	2,000
42	**Washington Arts Centre (Insticart)**	Financial assistance for developing a temporary, experimental Arts Centre to help with planning a permanent centre elsewhere.	10,000*
43	**Wearabout Theatre Company**	Complex project to establish a mobile theatre company to encourage community drama activities.	31,808*

Ref. No.	Name of Project	Summary Description	Cost to Experiment £
44	**Wearside Sub Aqua Club**	Equipment provided for a new club.	1,530
45	**Workingmen's Clubs' Fete**	2-day fete in 1974 to involve a wider group of participants.	3,901
46-51	**Youth Leisure Study**	Youth Leisure Committee established with funds for projects worked and determined by the group.	1,409
52	**Youth Theatre**	Small items of equipment for Sunderland Youth Theatre — young people interested in promoting youth drama.	41
		Total expenditure on projects	**206,868**

Note. *Money was also made available by other agencies towards the overall costs.

The Clwyd (Deeside) Experiment

locally known as
The Quality of Life Experiment

Local Sponsors
Clwyd County Council
Delyn Borough Council
Alyn and Deeside District Council
Welsh Arts Council
Sports Council for Wales

Experiment Area
Before Local Government Reorganisation
Flint Municipal Borough, Buckley, Connah's Quay, Holywell and
Mold Urban Districts, Hawarden and Holywell Rural Districts of
Flintshire.

After Local Government Reorganisation
Delyn Borough, Alyn and Deeside District of Clwyd.

Population
129,000 (December 1973)

Experiment Headquarters
Shire Hall, Mold, Clwyd

Local organisation

Quality of Life Steering Committee

Members

T M Haydn Rees CBE (Chairman)
Chief Executive, Clwyd County
Council

Cllr K Iball
Clwyd County Council

Cllr Walter Williams
Delyn Borough Council

G A McCartney
Chief Executive, Delyn Borough
Council

Cllr Eifion Jones
Alyn and Deeside District Council
(to February 1975)

Cllr E G Hett
Alyn and Deeside District Council
(from March 1975)

F N V Meredith
Chief Executive, Alyn and Deeside
District Council

Aneurin Thomas
Welsh Arts Council

Llion Williams
North Wales Arts Association

S G Griffiths
Sports Council for Wales

P Wallbank
Countryside Commission for Wales

P Roderick
Welsh Office

D V Leadbeater
Assessor for the Experiment

Steering Committee Panels

Research: Survey

S E Elmitt (Chairman)

Research: Organisations and Facilities

J Howard Davies (Chairman)
Director of Education, Clwyd County
Council

Research: Non-Participation Problems

G H Roberts (Chairman)

Arts

Glyn Davies (Chairman)
County Librarian, Clwyd County Council

Sports

G A Gearing (Chairman)
Recreation Officer, Alyn and Deeside
District Council

Youth and Community

Emyr Rowlands (Chairman)

Experiment Team

Director

S E Elmitt (to July 1974)

R H Williams (from July 1974)
Assistant Chief Executive, Clwyd County
Council

Assistants

W J Morgan

L Parker Davis

Evaluator

A Macbeath
Kelsterton College of Technology

Map 2.
Clwyd (Deeside) Experiment Area

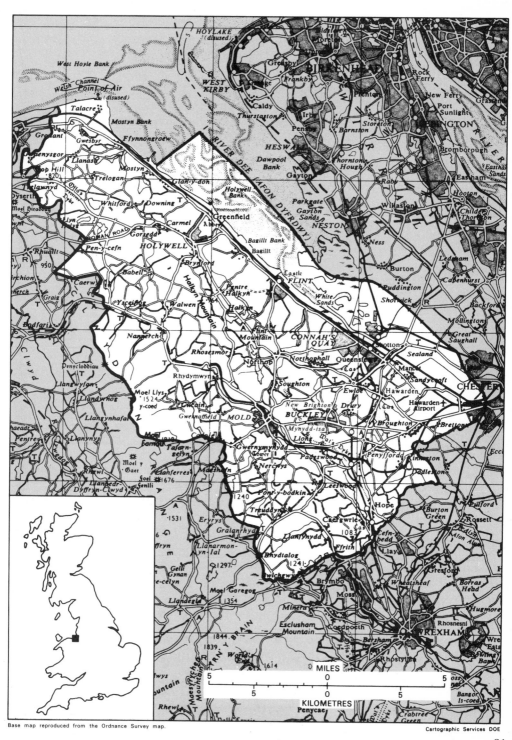

Base map reproduced from the Ordnance Survey map.

Cartographic Services DOE

81

The Clwyd (Deeside) Experiment

1   The 2 districts of Clwyd chosen for the Experiment area lie south
of the Dee estuary and are referred to locally as Deeside. They are
among the most heavily populated parts of North Wales and a large
proportion of the people alive in the estuary towns of Holywell, Flint
and Connah's Quay. The remainder live either in the small market
towns, villages and communities scattered in the valleys and hills to
the west and south or in the mixed urban/rural area around Buckley,
a former pottery and brick making centre, east of Mold, the county
centre. Deeside is growing rapidly in population. Many people have
moved into the area, particularly from Merseyside and the North West.
In some instances they have been absorbed by the existing communities but elsewhere in the smaller towns and villages they have out-
numbered the existing population and provision of community
facilities has not been able to keep pace with the growth of new
housing development. Steel, aircraft and rayon manufacture form
the main industrial employment in Deeside but a considerable number
of people travel to jobs in neighbouring Cheshire, for example to Chester
or Ellesmere Port. Thus the leisure pattern has to meet the needs
of industrial and rural living and of Welsh and English traditional
cultures. In providing for leisure in the County, emphasis was already
placed on the community — some sports halls were designed entirely
for community use including the Deeside Leisure Centre at Queens-
ferry built to international standards and opened in 1971. It was the
general policy of the County Education Department to allow school
premises (some already designated as community schools), to be freely
used for cultural activities. The new comprehensive Clwyd Arts Centre
was in the final stages of construction during the Experiment and
opened 2 months after it ended.

Setting up the Experiment

2   Following the invitation from the Welsh Office to take part in the
Experiments, T M Haydn Rees, the Clerk to Flintshire County Council
and later Chief Executive of the new Clwyd County Council, convened
a meeting of representatives from the local authorities and other interested bodies. In this part of the world it is natural for the local authorities
to take the lead in any new public enterprise and the meeting which took
place on 27 November 1973 agreed that its members should form the
Steering Committee of the Clwyd Experiment with the Chief Executive
as Chairman. The Quality of Life Steering Committee so formed eventually comprised members and officers of Clwyd County Council, the
Alyn and Deeside and Delyn District Councils and representatives of
the Welsh Arts Council, the North Wales Arts Association, the Welsh
Sports Council and the Countryside Commission.

Funds

3   In the funds for the Experiment locally, the 3 participating authorities agreed to match the central DES contribution (through the Welsh Arts Council) on the basis of £50,000 from the County Council and £25,000 from each District Council. The Welsh Sports Council provided £10,000 and together with the Welsh Office and other central funds mainly to meet research costs the total amounted to £251,000. During the course of the Experiment a number of other local donations were received towards individual projects including contributions from a number of Community/ Town Councils.

Staffing and Panels

4   The Steering Committee limited its function to that of determining policy and agreeing an overall programme. It met only 6 times during the Experiment and decisions made at its initial meeting not only set the pattern of its programme but also the way in which it was to be controlled. It was agreed that the Experiment should be carried out under local authority auspices making full use of the joint resources of both the county and the two districts but drawing also on voluntary help with the whole programme under a Director who would co-ordinate it. A full time Director, a local authority official about to retire, was appointed from the beginning of April 1974, but was obliged by illhealth to retire after the first few months and the task was taken on by a senior official from Clwyd in addition to his normal duties. He was helped by 2 assist-ants, 1 for an interim period and 1 full time. The headquarters of the Experiment was established in the Shire Hall at Mold since the County administration was closely identified with the Experiment. A Publicity Officer appointed for the Experiment (at first part time, later full time) worked closely with the County Information Services. Other staff were taken on for particular projects.

5   The Steering Committee also enlisted the help of 3 panels. Initially set up as Research Panels to collect information about the area, they were reconstituted later into Project Panels (chaired by officials from county and district) to promote arts, sports, youth and community activ-ities. The Panels worked in close association with the Director and helped to prepare and subsequently co-ordinate the whole programme. Once the programme framework and broad balance of expenditure as between arts, sports, and community projects had been agreed by the Steering Committee, it was left to the discretion of the Director and Panel Chairmen to make any necessary minor adjustments.

6   The decision to undertake preliminary research developed into a survey by the Kelsterton College of Technology at Connah's Quay. This was arranged by a lecturer in market research, later to become the part time Evaluator to the Experiment, using students, the college computer and other resources. The Evaluator was based at the college throughout the Experiment. Although working in association with the Director he

was not an integral part of his team. In a geographically scattered area, however, the fact that the Evaluator monitored individual projects helped to keep contact with the people involved. There was no feedback of evaluation reports but in the final stages the Evaluator took an active part in de-briefing sessions held by the Director.

Local criteria

7　The Steering Committee agreed at the outset that projects should complement the responsibilities of statutory authorities for leisure provision and that the programme should take account of the findings of the early research studies.

8　The results of the local studies made available by mid 1974 (see also Paper 23 in Volume 2) showed that a large proportion of the working population were shift workers, for whom normal participation in leisure activities was often difficult. Sports enthusiasts were on the whole satisfied with existing provision; because of the semi-rural character of the area some people found transport a problem. In general there seemed to be few latent interests for which provision was currently lacking. Taking these points into consideration, it was decided that the programme should aim to strengthen and expand existing provision but the Experiment generally should seek to act as a catalyst giving help and advice, guarantees against loss where appropriate, and acting overall as a sympathetic supporter of local initiative. In selecting projects the Steering Committee tried to avoid giving cash grants to organisations, preferring to assist in other ways, for example, by improving training facilities and equipment, by supplying goods and materials for clubs to 'do it themselves'. In borderline cases where local authorities had powers to help, it was decided that Experiment funds should not be used, for example, to improve playing fields or provide play equipment for children's playgrounds. But where the local authority could act as a catalyst to a new service which the Experiment would introduce this was regarded as acceptable. It was accepted that new building and applications for land acquisition would be excluded.

Experiment programme

9　The greater part of the work of preparing a programme, collecting ideas and developing projects was carried out by the Director and the 3 Panels in the summer of 1974. Most of the ideas for arts projects came from meetings and conferences held by the Arts Panel with drama and music societies, brass bands, art societies, film clubs, etc. The fact that the new Arts Centre was near completion was an obvious influence. Other ideas came from members of the Panel, for example, a mobile library service for housebound people. The Sports Panel held a series of meetings with Sports Hall managers, industrial social clubs and other groups which confirmed that the 2 districts were comparatively well served with sporting facilities. It was therefore agreed that the emphasis should be on developing, promoting and extending outdoor recreation and at the same time stimulating greater use of the existing indoor facilities and outdoor playing areas owned by the local authorities and industry. The sports programme was then developed along 4 main lines: creating and developing new clubs, organisations and activities; assisting existing clubs to increase participation (especially for the young); increasing the use of facilities and bringing them to notice by staging special events; and co-ordinating and publicising the range of facilities and programmes of activities which were available.

10   The Youth and Community Panel overlapped in many instances with the other 2 panels but in general it was responsible for provision for the disadvantaged members of society. It also sought ways in which people could be brought together and helped to identify with their local community, particularly in the areas which had received large numbers of new residents. The involvement of schools was particularly vital in this part of the programme. In the rural communities the school was often the only venue where activities could take place.

11   The main programme of projects and much of their development was worked out by September 1974 and finalised by the end of the first year of the Experiment. This left a full year in which to carry out the action and make ongoing arrangements. There were requests from other districts within Clwyd for assistance but projects were confined to Delyn and Alyn/Deeside, the 2 Districts of the Experiment. Nevertheless, in many of the projects, initiators, helpers and audiences came from well beyond the Experiment area as well as within it. All ideas submitted after the programme was agreed were in fact considered and most implemented within the scope of the 3 Panels' plans. Relatively few were rejected.

12   Altogether, something of the order of 140 projects were undertaken; 29 in the Arts, 51 Sports and 54 Community. In terms of expenditure nearly three-quarters of the project funds were allocated to the arts projects; the remainder in almost equal shares between sports and community projects.

Handling the projects

13   All ideas for projects were followed up by the Director and his assistants in discussions with the proposers. Arrangements to implement projects were made on a basis described by the Director as 'complete understanding and goodwill on both sides'. The methods adopted were highly flexible and paperwork was reduced to the minimum which helped to build up good relationships. It was left to the Director to keep expenditure on individual projects within the agreed estimates. Any purchases were made through local authority channels and equipment bought for clubs and societies was handed over (subject to conditions incorporated) in an exchange of letters, again handled by the Director and his team.

14   The whole programme of projects was co-ordinated by the Director and his team. But the 3 Panels and all local authority departments helped out with the task. In the organisation of projects the network went a great deal further involving, among others, Heads and staff of schools, the Principal and staff of Kelsterton College of Technology, Community Councils, voluntary organisations, Youth Officers, Youth Leaders and individuals.

15   The various organisers of projects were requested to submit quarterly reviews on progress. These were built up into a Progress Report submitted to the Steering Committee. The system also provided an opportunity to adjust certain projects if it appeared they were not meeting their objectives.

The projects

16   The Steering Committee, from the start, agreed on the importance of publicity, and reference has already been made to the appointment of a Publicity Officer. Publicity was used in the early stages and throughout to make the Experiment known by a variety of means — leaflets, posters, circulars, reports to press and radio, meetings, conferences and information booklets and publications. Meetings with organisations were usually relatively small — generally with Chairmen and Secretaries and were regarded as very successful. Public meetings in this Experiment were less successful; at most they attracted between 10 and 12 people.

17   The drama project was the most complex and ambitious and, in monetary terms, accounted for one half of the arts and nearly one quarter of the total expenditure on all projects. The majority of staff taken on in the course of the Experiment were appointed to work on various parts of this scheme — an Itinerant Drama Director to work with amateur companies and a group of Drama Advisers (movement specialist, designer and technical staff) to assist in the many productions put on by the County Drama Specialist Team and the Youth Theatre at different places in the two districts. Finally a professional company was appointed to establish what was hoped would be a more permanent and mobile community theatre. This called itself the 'Grass Roots Company'. The project was thus concerned with both amateur and professional drama and in part attempted co-operation between amateur and professionals.

18   The major role of the arts in this Experiment was also emphasised by the complex of projects in the fields of music and the visual arts. Local brass bands, choirs, music societies and amateur orchestras were helped in various ways, for example by provision of instruments, tuition and sheet music. This was supplemented by a specially arranged series of professional performances. In the visual arts, a picture lending library allowed people to enjoy art in their own homes while other projects encouraged local people to express themselves as artists and craftsmen. A Community Arts Centre was developed by a member of staff seconded part time from a local school in a converted community centre where

classes were started and clubs (Arts, Camera, Cine) could make their headquarters. The Arts Officer responsible did much to strengthen existing societies and form new ones (for example a Federation of Visual Arts). A mobile Community Cinema provided shows to many groups in various communities.

19   A wide range of local clubs (both arts and sports) was encouraged to extend their activities by providing better equipment and coaching and by arranging performances by professionals which would help to raise standards and increase membership. Wherever possible, materials rather than money grants were supplied so that clubs could construct their own facilities in their own way.

20   A series of projects — the Community Life Projects — was designed to stimulate interest and encourage participation in 17 different communities. In some instances this took the form of help for a particular group — in 2 or 3 simply providing equipment for old people — or for several clubs in a community. In others, various forms of help were given, for example, a student/adult orchestra was started, an information centre at a nature reserve was provided, clubs were helped with equipment, new clubs were instigated, events were organised, sometimes singly sometimes as a programme. In many instances help took the form of guarantees against loss. In the village of Treuddyn guarantees were given for a series of activities promoting Welsh culture including Welsh Drama , a Book Festival, a Threshing Fair, Eisteddfod, Noson Lawen, Cymanfa Ganu, Local and Popular Concerts. Community Festivals — a full week of events — were held in 2 centres — Connah's Quay and Holywell. At Mynydd Isa, a housing area with few facilities, a programme of activities and events was supported.

21   A feature of the Clwyd (Deeside) Experiment was close co-operation with existing community organisations and the creation of new ones. In the rural areas statutory Community Councils were involved in many projects, in some instances contributing financially; schools provided the venue and resources for many of the community projects; a District Sports Council was established in Alyn and Deeside to consolidate the progress made by sports projects. Everything possible was done to maximise the use of both buildings and facilities.

22   An equipment pool was built up and made available for loan throughout the 2 Districts and included items for both arts and sports activities. It included a Welsh harp and small libraries of folk, orchestral and brass band sheet music. Other items such as portable seating were part of the equipment to promote both indoor and outdoor activities. Camping and mountaineering equipment enabled the Probation Service to try out an outdoor camping experiment in the Snowdon area, a project which — it was anticipated — would be extended in the future.

23   A series of projects was mounted to help the disadvantaged. This included a mobile library service for the housebound and the completion of a magazine service to all blind people in the 2 Districts mostly by

volunteer effort while a Keep Fit Officer of the Keep Fit Association for Wales worked part timed organising acitivities for both able bodied and handicapped. A new sports club for the handicapped was established in 1 school where premises were adapted. As a result of this pilot scheme a further school was subsequently adapted in a similar way. A converted mini bus helped to meet the transport problems for such clubs.

24   Amongst other projects, swimming classes for shift workers were tried out and support given to a number of voluntary efforts in environmental improvement. Footway routes were negotiated and signposted. Two small surveys were undertaken, one of which was a survey of use of the sports centres in the 2 Districts. And, not least, help was given in forming new groups, clubs and societies both for sports and for arts, for example a Guitar Club, a Poetry Circle and a Community Theatre Club. Some of these — for instance a junior cricket league, a super swim team — were the result of the co-operation of clubs which had already received assistance. The help given in the new ventures was often in the form of guarantee against expenses of the first year, where fund-raising efforts were insufficient.

Arrangements for the future

25   In making ongoing arrangements 1 objective was to try and extend projects to other parts of the county wherever practicable. This applied particularly to projects which were started and expected to continue under the aegis of the local authority. But the Steering Committee were also concerned that the co-operation between County, Districts and Community Councils and the interest and self help generated in the communities in the area should not be lost. With a view to promoting necessary links between Local Authority and voluntary organisations and with the assistance of Clwyd Voluntary Services Committee a joint meeting of the Delyn and Alyn/Deeside Area Conferences of Community Councils was held at the end of the Experiment at which a paper was submitted for discussion on first suggestions about how this might be tackled. At the same time, as mentioned already, Alyn and Deeside had taken the lead in establishing a District Sports Council following joint meetings with local Community Councils and voluntary organisations on various activities. This Council expressed willingness to co-operate in a conference to consider a broad range of leisure activities. Arrangements were being made by the Experiment for similar discussions in Delyn.

Clwyd (Deeside) Experiment

Summary of projects (for fuller details see Paper 3 in Volume 2)

Ref. No.	Name of Project	Summary Description	Cost to Experiment £
1	**Arts Magazine**	Arts Magazine to publicise local cultural and community activities.	320
2-35	**Community Life**	Range of projects in various communities linked with making greater community use of schools and stimulating activities and interest in communities (rural and urban) where little or no provision existed.	5,195*
36	**Community Cinema**	Mobile film equipment and support to enable existing society develop film as an art form by providing shows to groups in the communities.	4,341
37-38	**Community Festivals at Connah's Quay and Holywell**	Activities, events, exhibitions promoted for 1 week in 2 centres. Organised by local effort with guarantee against loss.	3,370
39	**Council for Sport and Recreation in Alyn and Deeside**	Council of local authority and voluntary organisations established to develop interest and enthusiasm raised by the Experiment.	NIL
40-45	**Drama Project**	Interrelated projects to promote drama as a recreational activity for the community:— work of the county drama specialists developed by an augmented staff, help given to amateur companies and youth theatre, performances staged in different places in the community; workshops established; itinerant drama director appointed and professional community theatre group established based in Mold in Delyn Borough.	72,473*
46	**Festival of Movement and Dance**	Display of movement and dance by over 1,000 performers from arts and sports organisations, schools, etc.	1,525
47	**Film on the Experiment**	Film on the Experiment by Harlech Television Company, the Experiment contributing towards the cost.	2,000*

Ref. No.	Name of Project	Summary Description	Cost to Experiment £
48-51	**Footway Routes**	Two routeways worked out in each of the 2 Districts, signposted and routeway maps prepared and widely distributed.	5,035*
52-90	**Help to Existing and New Sports Clubs and Outdoor Recreation**	Equipment and other help given to existing clubs primarily aimed to develop training facilities. Wide range of activities covered. New groups were established — some the outcome of co-operative effort — and helped with initial expenses.	18,813
91	**Holiday for the Mentally Handicapped and Parents**	Two weeks holiday at a special residential school for senior handicapped children and 2 weeks of playgroup activity at 5 special schools for the younger handicapped.	2,096
92-93	**Improving Outdoor Sport and Recreation Facilities**	Permanent outdoor seating and floodlighting for athletics track provided to enable greater use particularly by schools.	5,132
94	**Improving Indoor Sport and Recreation Facilities**	New and wider variety of activities promoted and provided with equipment. Combined community activities at a school with the social facilities of a neighbouring leisure centre. Joint project with Alyn and Deeside District Council.	1,050*
95-96	**Industrial Archaeology**	Local museum established and housed in a local school in Buckley. Booklet published on former pottery industry of the area and industrial trail developed.	229
97	**Keep Fit Officer**	Part time Officer engaged to advise and assist with new keep fit courses and training of leaders.	1,076
98	**Mobile Library Service for the Housebound**	Regular mobile book selection and loan service introduced for the housebound. Two mobile units, running costs and driver/librarians supplied.	9,712
99-102	**Music Projects**		
99	*Brass Bands*	New instruments and professional tuition provided to help improve standards and train young players.	16,822*
100	*North Wales Brass Band Festival*	Support and equipment provided for festival held for the first time in Clwyd.	422

Ref. No.	Name of Project	Summary Description	Cost to Experiment £
101	*Choirs*	Tiered seating and portable staging provided and professional tuition made available.	3,984
102	*Amateur Music Making*	Amateur orchestras helped to promote concerts and given guarantees against loss. Two new orchestras established in local schools.	104
103-109	**New Arts Societies and Clubs**	A number of new groups and associations were given assistance with organisation, equipment, publicity and underwriting of initial costs. The groups included music, poetry, literature, drama, visual arts.	617
110-111	**Outdoor Equipment: Central Pools**	Two central pools of equipment to promote outdoor events and outdoor activities — the former organised and run by the College of Technology and the latter by Connah's Quay High School.	5,252
112	**Picture Lending Library**	Picture loan service initiated in 12 branch libraries. Works of local artists included.	10,434
113	**Professional Productions**	Series of visits by professional companies and individuals in drama, music, visual arts, literature arranged to encourage interest and high standards.	12,264
114	**Publicity**	Publicity officer appointed and wide variety of publicity methods tried out.	9,654
115	**Pursuits for Probationers — Outdoor Camping**	Series of weekend camps promoted in Snowdonia for young persons on probation and equipment provided (part of central pool of equipment).	1,370
116	**Sound Mazagine for the Blind**	Existing service extended to give 100 per cent coverage and made more frequent for all blind persons in the Experiment area.	1,306
117-118	**Sporting Facilities for the Handicapped**	School premises adapted, special transport provided so that handicapped people could take part in activities. Sports Club established.	4,235
119	**Sports Facilities for Shift Workers**	Swimming courses arranged at special times.	22

Ref. No.	Name of Project	Summary Description	Cost to Experiment £
120	**Survey: To Enquire Why so few Young People attend Music and Drama Events**	Groups of young people selected to attend events and record reactions. Survey only partially completed.	1,117
121	**Survey: Present Use of Sports Centres**	Six month survey of use of sports centres in the Experiment area.	2,879
122	**Transport to Events**	A ticket agency/transport service to enable people without convenient transport to attend events — a joint scheme with the local bus company.	626
123-124	**Visual Arts for the Community**	Community Centre adapted to become a Community Arts Centre and part time Community Arts Officer appointed to develop visual arts throughout the area.	9,503
125-128	**Voluntary Effort Supported**	Funding help to 3 'self-help' groups improving environment/building sport facilities.	1,658
129-140	**Welsh Culture Projects**	Financial underwriting for a Festival of Welsh Plays, a series of Welsh culture projects spaced over a year in a village; a Welsh harp purchased for general loan and equipment provided for the Welsh Youth Movement.	2,801
	Total expenditure on projects		**217,497**

Note. *Money was also made available by other agencies towards the overall costs.

The Stoke-on-Trent Experiment

locally known as
The Quality of Life Experiment

Local Sponsors
Stoke-on-Trent City Council
Staffordshire County Council
West Midlands Arts
West Midlands Sports

Experiment Area
Before Local Government Reorganisation
Stoke-on-Trent County Borough

After Local Government Reorganisation
Stoke-on-Trent District of Staffordshire

Population
259,000 (December 1973)

Experiment Headquarters
4 Mollart Street, Hanley, Stoke-on-Trent

Local organisation

Quality of Life Steering Committee

Members

H Naylor (Chairman)
A former Lord Mayor of Stoke-on-Trent

Cllr H Barks
Stoke-on-Trent City Council

Cllr J Monks-Neil
Stoke-on-Trent City Council

Cllr R Swann
Stoke-on-Trent City Council

S W Titchener
Town Clerk and Chief Executive,
Stoke-on-Trent City Council

Cllr Mrs M Stringer
Staffordshire County Council

Cllr G L Barber
Staffordshire County Council

G Sims
West Midlands Arts

B Moore
West Midlands Sports Council
(to March 1974)

J Sadler
West Midlands Sports Council
(March 1974 to April 1975)

D Francis
West Midlands Sports Council
(from May 1975)

L Finn
Stoke-on-Trent Sports Advisory Council

J Kent
Stoke-on-Trent Sports Advisory Council

Miss D Dent
Department of the Environment

P Cheeseman

R Cliffe

Professor L Fishman (from October 1974)

D Malkin

P Mountain (from December 1974)

Miss M Whalley

Dr E Duggan
Assessor for the Experiment

Quality of Life Sub-Committees

Young People

Mrs R E A Spry (Chairman)

Community

Mrs R E A Spry (Chairman)

*Mentally and Physically
Handicapped and Mentally Ill*

P Mountain (Chairman)

Elderly/Retired

D R Denton (Chairman)

Experiment Team

Director

D R Denton

Assistant Director

Mrs R E A Spry

Evaluator

Miss A M Thompson

Map 3.
Stoke-on-Trent Experiment Area

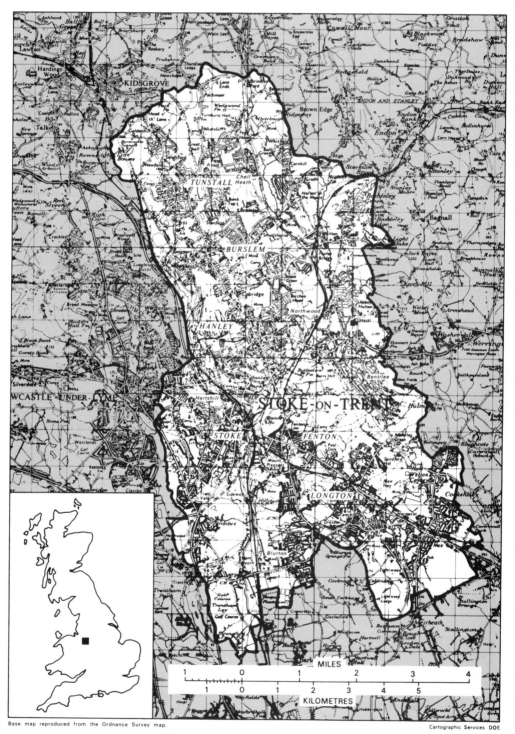

Base map reproduced from the Ordnance Survey map.

Cartographic Services DOE

The Stoke-on-Trent Experiment

1   The City of Stoke-on-Trent remains in essence an amalgam of the former 6 Pottery towns extending from Tunstall in the north through Burslem, Hanley (the principal shopping centre) Stoke and Fenton to Longton in the south. Although a single local authority since 1910, it is still widely known as 'the Potteries' and each town retains its own distinctive character and community interest. Midway between Birmingham and Manchester, Stoke-on-Trent is strongly independent, holding aloof from the West Midlands region of which it is nominally a part and regarding itself as the natural centre for North Staffordshire, rural and urban areas alike. Coal, clay and pottery, from fine china to earthenware, have long been the City's lifeblood. Names such as Wedgwood, Doulton and Minton, well known in this country since the eighteenth century, are internationally famous today. With many coal tips, clay workings and pot banks scattered throughout its built up area, Stoke-on-Trent is now carrying through a major programme of land reclamation which is adding substantially to the open space for leisure use within its boundaries. Interest is now being focussed on preserving the best features of the City's heritage with industrial museums, industrial trails and canal improvements, and efforts are also being made to promote the City as an international tourist centre. It joins with its neighbour, Newcastle-under-Lyme, to run an annual festival aiming principally to develop interest in the arts. It has a professional repertory theatre and a legacy of 7 town halls (2 in Burslem) where concerts and other activities can take place. Two league teams Stoke City and Port Vale are indications of the scale of Stoke-on-Trent's interest in sport. At the beginning of the Experiment a large swimming pool was nearing completion. This was intended to form part of an indoor sports and leisure complex still in the planning stages.

Setting up the Experiment

2   Of the Local Sponsors of this Experiment, the City Council took the lead in setting up a steering group responsible for framing policy and carrying it out. Known locally as the Quality of Life Committee, it was chaired by Harold Naylor, much respected as a former Lord Mayor and Alderman of Stoke-on-Trent. Members of the Committee included representatives from the 4 Local Sponsors (Stoke-on-Trent City and Staffordshire County Councils, West Midlands Arts and the West Midlands Sports Council), the Stoke-on-Trent Local Advisory Sports Council, Keele University and other cultural, community and trade interests.

3   Financial services for the Experiment were provided by Stoke City Council, who themselves contributed £40,000. With support from the central sponsoring departments and £5,000 contributed by Staffordshire County Council, the Experiment had £245,000 at its disposal.

4   The Experiment was launched at a conference arranged by the City to which it had invited a wide range of people covering leisure interests in both City and County. Publicity from this meeting and an appeal for suggestions on Radio Stoke by the Chairman of the Quality of Life Committee brought in the first ideas for projects.

5   The effects of local government reorganisation were felt particularly keenly in Stoke. The City lost its county borough status and control of education and social services passed to Staffordshire County Council. This meant a period of considerable readjustment and contraction. As a result the City was able to give only limited support in the first few months of the Experiment and there was inevitably some marking of time until the newly appointed Director and Assistant Director were able to take up duty in the spring of 1974. Some of the momentum following the original announcement was lost during this period and when activities were resumed the Steering Committee had to make a fresh start in publicising the Experiment. Local press publicity remained something of a problem throughout the first half of the Experiment. Perhaps because domestic rate increases were a particularly sensitive local issue at that time, the press tended to stress the amount of money available for the Experiment rather than the purpose to which it was directed and the opportunities which it offered to people.

The first steps

6   Once their staff, with clerical support, were in post the Steering Committee decided to get action started quickly. From ideas already before them they agreed to follow up 3 major proposals — the development of a Burslem Leisure Centre as a joint project with Stoke City Council, a proposal by the local Victoria Theatre for an intensive community theatre programme throughout the City and the establishment of a community centre at the independently run Gladstone Pottery Museum. For these schemes they provisionally allocated some 40 per cent of the Experiment funds. Before the Committee as a whole got to work a preliminary planning group had discussed ideas for programming and some members now pressed for an outline programme against which future proposals could be considered rather than on merit as they came up. Concern about determining a future programme was also linked with the problem of working through a large committee. There were 18 voting members but attendance which included representatives from various interested departments of Stoke City Council often totalled as many as 30 or 40 people most of whom joined actively in discussion. A suggestion for setting up a committee to sift proposals was considered but turned down since the Steering Committee wished to be kept fully in the picture about projects. In the event, the Committee decided to structure its approach by setting up a number of sub-committees to act as 'think tanks' and to advise on the best way of allocating the remaining resources. The sub-committees were also intended to draw a wider range of people mainly from the voluntary sector into the workings of the Experiment.

7   Sub-committees were set up to consider the needs of elderly people; young people generally; the community and the mentally and physically handicapped or ill. The Steering Committee chose this client-group approach in the belief that it was more realistic than the traditional way of thinking of leisure in terms of art, sport and recreation. The hope was that as a result projects would come forward which would straddle conventional boundaries in the leisure field. In addition, a number of ad hoc working parties were set up to handle issues which arose in the fields of music, sports, area arts and the major Burslem Leisure Centre project. There was also an inter-denominational religious group. Every sub-committee and working party included 1 Steering Committee member. The role of the sub-committees developed during the course of the Experiment and some took on a management function. The Sub-Committee dealing with the Elderly grew into an Older Persons Welfare Committee; the Community Sub-Committee took on the management and development of Stoke Video Group, and the Sub-Committee for the Physically and Mentally Handicapped became the Management Committee for the Community Transport Scheme.

8   The Steering Committee met monthly from April 1974. The Experiment Headquarters was first established in Council premises near the Town Hall in Stoke but in January 1975 a move was made to premises near the popular shopping centre of Hanley. This situation proved far more accessible and the Experiment Centre quickly became a focal point and regular meeting place for a wide range of organisations in the leisure field to whom the Experiment's staff were also able to offer advice, support and secretarial assistance.

Handling the projects

9   Most ideas, proposals and applications were considered as a first step by the officers and discussed with the proposers. A list of criteria was drawn up by them as a basis for selecting projects. Accepted by the Steering Committee without discussion, these criteria were incorporated in a standard letter sent to anyone enquiring about the Experiment. Proposers were asked to state their aim in making the proposal and whom it would benefit. Proposals were submitted to the Committee on a simple form for consideration. Generally, proposers, whether individuals or representatives of a group, attended the Committee meeting to support their proposal. Where the proposal was accepted in principle or referred back for further discussion, Experiment Officers, working parties and sub-committees continued the process and the final stage was the preparation of a worksheet giving details of the organisation, administrative responsibility, financing and an outline of the evaluation to be carried out. Once approved by the Steering Committee, action could go ahead. All the main projects were decided by the Committee but small projects were initiated with the Chairman's approval within an agreed budget.

10   A system of evaluation was worked out by the Project Evaluator (who joined the Team in the summer of 1974) with guidance from Professor Leslie Fishman of Keele University, a co-opted member of the Steering Committee. Most of the main projects were evaluated but while accepting the need for evaluation as a condition of the Experiment, the Committee did not lay great stress on this aspect in deciding on projects. The Evaluator was left to build in her requirements in the best way possible. Nor did the Committee call for any feedback from the evaluation process.

Publicising the Experiment

11   Awakening public interest and drawing in new ideas proved difficult, particularly after the initial loss of momentum. The Steering Committee were concerned about the 'low key image of the Experiment', as it was described by a public relations consultant whom they called in jointly with West Midlands Arts to advise both on the potential for a local Arts Council and on general publicity methods. They also felt some sensitivity about local criticism that projects already planned were linked in one way or another with Committee members' interests. A special effort was made to extend publicity through the media. Radio Stoke had been helpful throughout and press coverage became more sympathetic in the latter half of the Experiment after representatives of the press had been invited to attend Steering Committee meetings. The Director and Assistant Director generated a great deal of interest by their efforts in meeting individuals, groups and associates, following up leads, and bringing together people with common areas of activities. A list was built up of all voluntary organisations in the City and this was used selectively to inform groups about projects likely to be of interest to them, in the hope that it would lead to a feedback of ideas. At the half way mark of the Experiment, a leaflet was compiled and widely circulated again with a view to arousing interest, attracting ideas and discovering need.

The projects

12   In total the Stoke-on-Trent Experiment promoted 74 projects. The 3 largest all in one way or another involved an extension of leisure opportunities to a broader cross section of the population. Of these the conversion of Burslem Old Town Hall into an all-purpose leisure centre took longest to negotiate. Architecturally and historically it is an important building and the City Council had long wanted to put it to good use but had been deterred by the difficulties and expense. An offer by the Steering Committee to share the cost of conversion finally provided the impetus necessary but it was only after considerable doubts and delays, as well as solving practical problems of heating and management that the decision was taken to go ahead and some Committee members continued to feel concerned about the scale of expenditure in relation to the Experiment funds. Under the agreement finally reached with Stoke-on-Trent City Council, conversion and management of the Leisure Centre became

a venture in partnership, the Council undertaking to continue the Centre after the Experiment had been concluded under a management committee on which voluntary interests would be represented, though in the minority. Administrative arrangements and actual conversion work took longer than anticipated but the Centre was finally opened on 14 November 1975 by Mr Denis Howell MP, Minister for Sport and Recreation. At a cost of some £70,000, shared between the Local Authority and the Steering Committee it provided the northern part of Stoke-on-Trent with a centre for concerts, exhibitions and rehearsal facilities; for indoor sports such as badminton and weight lifting, where courses such as pottery and painting could be held and where clubs and other voluntary organisations could meet. It was also intended to develop it as a centre for urban studies for Stoke-on-Trent as a whole.

13   The Community Centre project at the Gladstone Pottery Museum in Longton (selected Museum of the Year in 1976) involved the conversion of part of the old pottery warehousing into premises which were used in a flexible way for clubs for children, classes, meetings and exhibitions. A Community Leader was appointed to develop activities working in collaboration with the Museum Director. Staffordshire County Council agreed to sponsor her from the latter part of 1975.

14   The third major project was the Community Theatre scheme carried out by the professional and well known Victoria Theatre Company. The 'Vic' had already started to experiment in this field but the Quality of Life Experiment provided an opportunity to intensify the work and extend effort to all parts of the City. With intensive efforts by the existing theatre personnel augmented by additional actors, actresses and administrative staff and with additional premises, and the use of a van, the Company mounted a comprehensive 15-month programme. Altogether they put on 240 performances including 12 different road shows and 3 children's participation shows and took them to a wide range of audiences in old peoples' clubs and clubs for the young and the handicapped as well as pubs, schools, church halls, parks and playgrounds. The Company also prepared and ran a number of courses in their own premises designed mainly to help social and community workers and teachers to follow up and develop interest awakened by the road shows.

15   The remaining work of the Experiment can be divided into 4 broad fields of endeavour: the arts, sport and outdoor recreation, activities for children, and activities for the handicapped and disadvantaged. In the arts field, in addition to the large Victoria Theatre project, the Experiment provided a guarantee against loss to the Stoke and Newcastle Festival Board for 2 of their projects — the Autumn Cluster and a Celebrity Concert. A study of the potential for a local arts organisation and manager for the arts was commissioned from a consultant and following this an Area Arts Officer was appointed in partnership with West Midlands Arts to stimulate interest in the arts in both Stoke-on-Trent and Newcastle-under-Lyme. Other arts projects included the sponsorship of a poetry magazine, lunchtime concerts, and encouragement of the

popular film-making movement based at the North Staffordshire Polytechnic.

16   On the sports side, activities encompassed the development of coaching for young people, support for newly formed clubs, and help to existing clubs to extend their activities to wider sections of the population. Among the sports assisted were rugby football, orienteering and sky-diving (parachute jumping) and sub aqua. A marked feature of the Stoke-on-Trent Experiment was the provision of activities for children. A total of some £34,000 was spent directly on projects for their benefit; concern ranged from pre-school play groups through the leisure problems of the school holidays to the constructive use of leisure by teenagers. In addition to action projects, an ambitious and successful survey was carried out of school-leavers from 2 schools in the City, and an imaginative School Leaver's Leisure Guide produced on the basis of its findings. Projects for the disadvantaged included support for leisure ventures among the elderly, a great deal of attention to the problems of handicapped people and efforts to make contact with some of the most deprived groups in the City to see if constructive help could be given through the medium of leisure activities. One consequence of the strong 'localist' tradition in the Potteries was that the Steering Committee made a conscious effort to provide a balance in projects between the different parts of the 'Six Towns'. A number of projects, by their very nature, tended to be located in Hanley which is the most central of the Six Towns. On the other hand, projects such as the Victoria Theatre Road Show and the North Staffordshire Playbus travelled throughout the City.

17   In general, organisation of projects was carried out by the proposers, whether an individual, club, society or organisation. For some projects additional paid help was employed, for example, extra actors and administrators for the Victoria Theatre, a play co-ordinator to develop play activities, staff for the Playbus and a community leader for the Gladstone Centre, but the work of these employees was supplemented by a great deal of voluntary effort. The local authority was also directly involved in some projects which it carried out with its own staff, in particular the conversion of Burslem Town Hall and the conversion of reclaimed derelict land for unusual leisure activities — a 'trim park' and a children's zoo in semi-natural surroundings.

Ongoing arrangements

18   Action in this Experiment continued until the last meeting of the Steering Committee in May 1976 but ongoing arrangements had been under discussion with Stoke-on-Trent, Staffordshire, and the other Local Sponsors since the beginning of the year. The County, from the latter part of 1975, had sponsored the Community Leader at the Gladstone Centre and agreed to give support for the Playbus. Stoke City Council were also to sponsor some other projects concerned with play as well as continuing support for others, such as the Burslem Leisure Centre, in which they had a direct interest. These projects were assured of continu-

ance for a further year, but subject to review in 1977. No special provision was made for projects for the elderly, such as 'Life Begins at 60' and 'Leisure in Retirement', the County taking the view that its Youth and Community Service was making significant provision in this field. However, it promised the co-operation of the area officers and also undertook to refer these projects to the Standing Conference of Voluntary Service Work Organisation and the Beth Johnson Foundation.

19   West Midland Arts took over the surveillance of some of the arts projects entrusting them to the Area Arts Officer who was continuing beyond the end of the Experiment to complete his contract. It had been hoped that the Experiment Centre would continue to function under the aegis of the local Voluntary Services Council, providing headquarters for them and remaining available to those groups which had used the premises during the Experiment. Arrangements for this broke down and West Midlands Arts took over the lease, using the centre as a base for the Area Arts Officer with loan arrangements to be agreed with the Voluntary Services Council. The Victoria Theatre were to endeavour to continue community drama work though without any special allocation of funds for the purpose. The Local Sports Council would continue their interest in sports projects.

20   The Chairman and many members of the Steering Committee pressed in the last meetings for the continuance of the committee in some form in the future perhaps to consider and advise on recreation generally. The City Council decided against supporting this proposal. At the final meeting of the Committee the Town Clerk agreed to investigate the matter further. Consideration has since been deferred to await publication of this report.

Stoke-on-Trent Experiment

Summary of projects (for fuller details see Paper 3 in Volume 2)

Ref. No.	Name of Project	Summary Description	Cost to Experiment £
1	**Adventure Playground at Chell Heath**	Improvement to a hut to make it usable in winter and evenings and more attractive to a variety of organisations.	1,704
2	**Area Arts Officer**	Special Officer appointed to support and advise existing activities, stimulate new activity and investigate the feasibility of setting up a local arts council.	10,777* (see also project 15)
3	**Bentilee Day Nursery**	Funds to launch a nursery for 'under-5s' to be run by qualified staff. Help needed to provide toys, a storage hut and fencing.	199
4	**Burslem Leisure Centre**	Old Town Hall converted into leisure centre for multi-purpose use, including arts, sports and educational activities.	33,184*
5-11	**Community Festivals**	Seven local festivals in 1975 given help of various kinds. Only 2 required financial help.	1,137
12	**Community Theatre of the Victoria Theatre**	Professional Company augmented to take theatre into the community. In an intensive 15 month programme Road Show performances were undertaken in wide variety of venues throughout the City and a series of courses promoted.	42,640
13	**Community Transport Scheme**	Purchase of a special vehicle to transport handicapped, elderly and others.	7,529
14	**Esperanto Congress**	Grant towards expenses of organising a Congress on Railway Esperantism.	50
15	**Experiment Centre — Mollart St.**	Premises near to Hanley town centre leased and adapted for use as Experiment Headquarters. Continued use as base for Area Arts Officer for post Experiment period. (conversion and running costs during Experiment) + (towards running costs post Experiment)	3,496 2,850

Ref. No.	Name of Project	Summary Description	Cost to Experiment £
16	**Film: 'Power Over The Clay'**	Local documentary with over 350 local people involved. Shown widely in Stoke-on-Trent and elsewhere.	3,082
17	**Film: 'I Want To Be Famous'**	Some support for a practical demonstration in film-making.	450*
18	**Gladstone Centre, at Gladstone Pottery Museum**	Large area of museum converted for multi-purpose use jointly with the Gladstone Museum.	20,660*
19	**Hanley Youth Project — London Road Shop**	Equipment for a shop converted into an informal meeting place, especially for teenagers.	481
20	**Home-School-Child -Parent Link**	Encouragement in communication and good relationships between home and school.	686
21	**Islamic Cultural Centre**	Funds to convert a chapel into a Centre to improve relations between immigrant and other communities and to introduce Islamic culture. Intended to be non-political, non-sectarian.	4,004*
22	**Mount Pleasant Community Holiday Projects**	Two week playscheme in church hall. Children, parents and elderly all catered for.	393
23-26	**Music Projects**		
23	*Lunchtime Concerts*	Professional lunchtime concerts to encourage participation in music. Near capacity audiences.	481
24	*'Do it Yourself' Messiah*	An unrehearsed performance by local singers and musicians with some professional lead.	1,169
25	*Music and Drama Festival*	Competitive event, including classes in music, speech and drama.	(included in project 24)
26	*Celebrity Concert*	Celebrity Concert, featuring Daniel Barenboim and the English Chamber Orchestra.	1,301*
27	**North Staffordshire Boat Club**	Equipment to expand boat club activities, particularly its training capacity.	793
28	**North Staffordshire Playbus**	Mobile playgroup facilities in a converted bus.	9,739*

Ref. No.	Name of Project	Summary Description	Cost to Experiment £
29	**North Staffordshire Sub Aqua Club**	Equipment to expand existing club's training facilities.	288
30	**Old Longtonians Rugby Union Foot-ball Club**	Conversion of old farm buildings for a local rugby club. Experiment contributed funds. Club members undertook most of the conversion work.	3,000*
31	**Orienteering**	Formation of local orienteering club.	170
32	**Pets Corner — Finney Gardens**	Pets corner in semi-natural environment to provide a facility in area of urban development.	4,000*
33-36	**Play Projects**		
33	*Play Symposium*	Day Conference for people associated with play in Stoke-on-Trent.	20
34	*Play Council: Appointment of Play Co-ordinators*	Paid staff employed to promote and co-ordinate play activities in Stoke-on-Trent working to the Play Council.	7,965
35	*Playmates Schemes*	Paid playleaders in parks or other open space, with some limited equipment provided.	1,028
36	*Holiday Project for Handicapped Children*	Two-week scheme to relieve parents of handicapped children and give children a change of environment. New scheme in Stoke-on-Trent.	168
37-38	**Poetry Magazine and Visual Arts Project.**	Local poetry magazine published and visual arts promoted.	1,987
39	**Publicity**	Public Relations Consultant engaged to consider scope for a manager for the Arts for an area arts council and publicity for the Experiment.	200
40	**Reclaimed Open Space — Trim Park**	Fitness trail to encourage greater use of land reclaimed for open space.	750
41	**Refocus**	A month of events refocussing people's attention to activities now available as a result of the Experiment.	304
42	**Rent-a-bike**	Project to encourage cycling and awareness of local amenities especially amongst families.	707*

Ref. No.	Name of Project	Summary Description	Cost to Experiment £
43	**Repertory Players Stoke-on-Trent**	Conversion of church hall to provide additional capacity for amateur theatre company.	1,604
44	**Riding for the Disabled**	Riding lessons for handicapped children.	203
45	**School Leavers, Survey and Leisure Guide**	Survey to discover recreational needs of school leavers. Leisure guide published for them.	2,997
46-49	**Senior Citizen Projects**		
46	*Residential Courses for the Elderly*	Two residential courses to introduce retired people to a range of leisure activities.	468
47	*Life Begins at 60*	Day-time activities for elderly in different parts of Stoke-on-Trent.	1,106
48	*Leisure in Retirement Guide*	Booklet on all aspects of retired persons' leisure and on other benefits available.	575
49	*Tunstall Day Centre*	Help to equip a new day centre for the elderly.	
50	**Six Towns Press**	Provision of low cost printing services for voluntary and other organisations.	214
51	**Ski-ing for All**	Equipment for club to expand training facilities.	1,047
52-64	**Small Projects**	A total of 13 small projects helped in a variety of ways including administration and publicity, using the Experiment's circulation system and its Centre as a post box and meeting place.	674
65	**Sports Coaching**	Coaching courses in different sports and facilities improved at a local athletics stadium.	5,309
66	**Staffordshire Sports Sky-divers (Stoke Group)**	Equipment for local club to expand training activities.	3,933
67	**Stoke and New-castle Festival — Autumn Cluster**	Guarantee against loss for a series of first class artistic events covering drama, modern music, dancing and art.	2,600

Ref. No.	Name of Project	Summary Description	Cost to Experment £
68	'Time to care' with BBC Radio Stoke	Six programmes on the development of community care groups.	900
69	Training Course Fund	Funds to assist individuals to attend training courses.	91
70	Transport for the Handicapped (Stallington Hospital)	Chair lift contributed for a special vehicle being purchased by a voluntary group from fund raising effort.	417
71	Trentham Rugby Club	Improvements to club premises.	1,100
72	Under 10's Leisure	Worker to promote leisure activities amongst children in a deprived area.	5,016
73	Visual Aids Service	Do-it-yourself project with video equipment. Familiarisation courses run.	3,126
74	Wind Orchestra — Longton/Fenton	Instruments purchased to expand an existing wind band for school children.	1,259
	Total expenditure on projects		**200,596**

Note: *Money was also made available by other agencies towards the overall costs.

The Dumbarton Experiment

locally known as
The Quality of Life Experiment

Local Sponsors
Dumbarton, Helensburgh, Cove and Kilcreggan Burgh Councils,
Helensburgh and Vale of Leven District Councils
   (later Dumbarton District Council)
Dunbartonshire Education Committee
   (later Strathclyde Regional Education Committee)
Scottish Arts Council
Scottish Sports Council

Experiment Area
Before Local Government Reorganisation
Dumbarton, Helensburgh, Cove and Kilcreggan Burghs,
Helensburgh and Vale of Leven Districts of Dunbartonshire

After Local Government Reorganisation
Dumbarton District in Strathclyde Region

Population
78,000 (December 1973)

Experiment Headquarters
92 College Street, Dumbarton
(This also served as the Dumbarton Neighbourhood Group Office.
Other Neighbourhood offices were in Alexandria (Vale of Leven), and
in Helensburgh.)

Local organisation

Dumbarton District (previously West Dunbartonshire) Community Development Advisory Board (†)

Members

Cllr Duncan Mills (Chairman)

C Mc Gregor (1) **(Vice Chairman)**
Vale of Leven District Council

Cllr I McDuff (1)
Dumbarton Burgh Council/co-opted

** **L MacKinnon** (1)
Dumbarton Burgh Council

Cllr P McCann (1)
Dumbarton Burgh Council/Dumbarton
District Council

E Young
Dunbarton Education Committee/co-opted

** **P F Drake** (1)
Dunbarton Education Committee

Cllr J Blair (1)
Dunbarton Education Committee/
Dumbarton District Council

J A Steven (1)
Dunbarton Education Committee/
co-opted

F Irvine (1)
Vale of Leven District Council

I Owen (1)
Vale of Leven District Council/
Dumbarton District Council

Mrs W Edwards (1)
Helensburgh Burgh Council/co-opted

Cllr J Graham (1)
Helensburgh Burgh Council/
Dumbarton District Council

** **R McKay** (1)
Helensburgh Burgh Council

R MacQuarrie
Helensburgh District Council/co-opted

Cllr F Kane
Helensburgh District Council/co-opted

Mrs M MacDonald
Helensburgh District Council/co-opted

** **Mrs C Allan** (1)
Helensburgh District Council

** **A Erskine** (1)
Helensburgh District Council

** **J Allen** (1)
Cove & Kilcreggan Burgh Council

** **C W Jackson** (1)
Cove & Kilcreggan Burgh Council

C Hanley (1)
Scottish Arts Council

A Dunbar (Assessor) (1)
Scottish Arts Council

** **L Tatham** (1)
Scottish Sports Council

N J Gibbs.
Scottish Sports Council

** **K L Gill** (1)
Scottish Sports Council

J Kidd (Assessor) (1)
Scottish Education Department

J Murray Allan (Assessor) (1)
Dunbartonshire Education Department/
Strathclyde Education Department

D MacCalman (Assessor) (1)
Scottish Education Department (also
Assessor for the Experiment)

Cllr J Hannah
Dumbarton District Council

Cllr T McArthur
Dumbarton District Council

** **Cllr G Wilmshurst**
Dumbarton District Council

Cllr N Glen
Dumbarton District Council

Cllr J Irvine
Strathclyde Regional Council

† List of members taken from the final local
report of the Advisory Board.

Cllr M Turner
Strathclyde Regional Council

** **Rev M Mair** (1)
Co-opted

J Brown
Co-opted

Cllr I Leitch
Co-opted

Cllr J Mackenzie
Co-opted

A Russell
Co-opted

Mrs J Harrison
Co-opted

W McNaught
Co-opted

R Summers
Co-opted

Honorary Officers

Administrator
C Douse

Finance Officer
** **D Blackie**

Finance Officer
P K Mill

Neighbourhood Development Groups
(see page 119)

Experiment Team

Director
P B L Stott

Area (Dumbarton) & Arts Co-ordinator
O Bennett

Area (Vale of Leven) & Environment Co-ordinator
Miss J Skinner (to June 1975)

Area (Helensburgh) & Sports Co-ordinator
Mrs M Stewart (to January 1975)

Mrs M Weir (from January 1975)

Evaluator

J Cassidy
University of Strathclyde

(1) Members who constituted the original Advisory Board.

** Members who retired or resigned and were replaced.

Neighbourhood Development Groups †

Dumbarton

Cllr I MacDuff
Advisory Board

** Rev G Nugent (Chairman)
Archdiocese of Glasgow

Rev A Noonan
Archdiocese of Glasgow

** Rev M Mair
Dumbarton Presbytery

Rev W N F Niven
Dumbarton Presbytery

Mrs T Abraham
Arts/Sports Groups

P Leddy
Arts/Sports Groups

H L Freeman
Arts/Sports Groups

Mrs A Ellis
Arts/Sports Groups

W Tevendale
Trades Council

Mrs M McGregor
Schools

R Macdonald
Community Education Service

J Brown (Chairman)
Chamber of Commerce

J Rutherford
Social Work Department

** I Owen
Civic Amenities Department
(Dumbarton District Council)

R Armstrong
Co-opted

R MacGregor
Co-opted

Helensburgh

Cllr J Graham (Chairman)
Advisory Board

** Rev J McCabe
Archdiocese of Glasgow

Rev R A Fox
Dumbarton Presbytery

R S Wilkie
Arts/Sports Groups

J S Grogan
Arts/Sports Groups

Dr G T Morrice
Arts/Sports Groups

S J Dorey
Arts/Sports Groups

Mrs J G Allan
Schools

J Leask
Youth and Community Service

W McClure
Social Work Department

** I Owen
Civic Amenities Department
(Dumbarton District Council)

Miss W De'Ath
Co-opted

K Mitchell
Co-opted

Mrs R McKerron
Co-opted

R Mair
Co-opted

† List of members taken from the final local
report of the Advisory Board

Vale of Leven

C McGregor
Advisory Board

Rev D Gallagher
Archiocese of Glasgow

Rev G S Smith
Dumbarton Presbytery

** **J Gardner**
Arts/Sports Groups

Mrs M McAulay
Arts/Sports Groups

Miss M Galbraith
Arts/Sports Groups

A S Davis
Arts/Sports Groups

N S McEwan
Trades Council

A I Henderson (Chairman)
Schools

A J Blackie
Youth and Community Service

A G Gillespie
Social Work Department

** **I Owen**
Civic Amenities Department
(Dumbarton District Council)

Mrs E Black
Co-opted

** Members who retired or resigned and were replaced.

Map 4.
Dumbarton Experiment Area

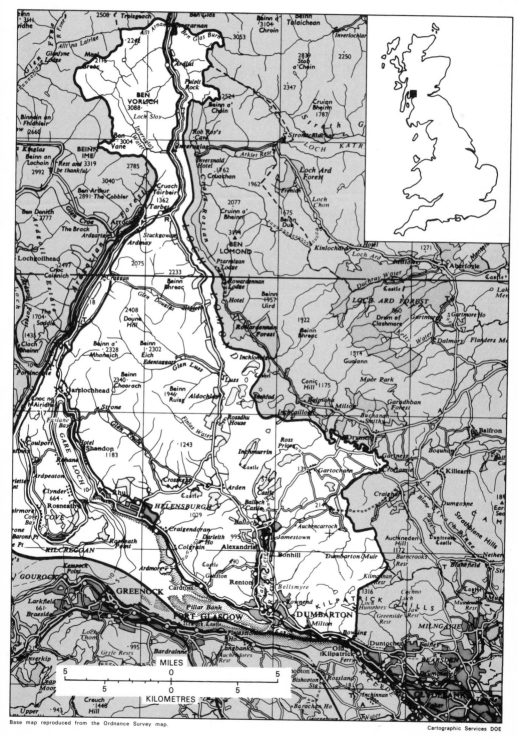

Base map reproduced from the Ordnance Survey map.

Cartographic Services DOE

The Dumbarton Experiment

1   Dumbarton District, to the west of Glasgow and north of the Clyde, is an area of contrasting geographical features and social characteristics. It is roughly triangular in shape, with the Clyde as the base and the northern apex at Arrochar. To the west it is bounded by Loch Long and to the north east by Loch Lomond and the Vale of Leven. For the greater part, it is an area of sea and fresh water lochs, steep craggy hills and deep glens. Of its population of 78,000 — the smallest of the 4 Experiments — three-quarters are concentrated in 3 urban centres, the town of Dumbarton which had been a Royal Burgh since 1222 but lost its burgh status with the reform of local government in 1975, the Vale of Leven which is a series of urban communities (Bonhill, Renton, Alexandria, Jamestown and Balloch) and Helensburgh which, despite its naval base, is mainly a residential resort town, 'the garden city of the Firth of Clyde'. Industrial development is mainly concentrated in Dumbarton and the Vale of Leven. In the past it was mainly shipbuilding, now it is light engineering and allied industries, whisky distilling and bonding.

2   Socially, there are sharp contrasts and unemployment is spread throughout the District. Of 28 wards considered in the West Central Scotland Plan of 1974[1], 5 in Helensburgh and District, 1 in the Vale of Leven and 1 in Dumbarton were classified as among the least deprived. Three wards, all in the Vale of Leven, were among the most deprived. The area is linked to Glasgow by both suburban and main line rail. Many of the employed travel daily to work in the city. The retired form a relatively large proportion of the population in the Helensburgh area and an increasing proportion in the town of Dumbarton.

3   The people of Dumbarton District have a strong sense of heritage and a community spirit which is tempered with a degree of rivalry between Dumbarton, the Vale of Leven and Helensburgh. Indeed, the instinct for local identification goes further and is often associated with quite small communities, neighbourhoods, villages, even housing estates. Many have established local Community Associations, encouraged by the Youth and Community Service. The leisure pattern in the District is equally varied. Countryside, loch or riverside activities are everywhere within reach and Glasgow with all that it has to offer is easily accessible to those with money and transport. For the local leisure needs, a range of facilities have been provided and there are Community Education Centres which serve all ages for 7 days a week in most but not all areas of the District. Dumbarton has its Civic Theatre. The Clyde Naval Base in the Helensburgh area makes some of its facilities accessible to the public.

---

[1] 'West Central Scotland Plan': by the West Central Scotland Planning Team, Consultants — Colin Buchanan and Partners and Professor K J W Alexander, August 1974.

The local structure

4   Following the invitation to take part in the Experiment, extended from the Scottish Education Department on 23 October 1973, a Local Group — the Dumbarton District Community Development Advisory Board — was established through the Dunbartonshire Education Committee. The first meeting of the Advisory Board took place on 13 February 1974, the interval in the Board's description 'representing the period which it took for consultation and negotiations in what was a very complicated situation to take place'.

5   The members of the Advisory Board were originally drawn from the sponsoring local authorities and arts and sports organisations but allowance was made for up to 6 co-options. As first set up, the Board consisted of 3 representatives of the Dunbartonshire Education Committee, 3 representatives (2 members and 1 official) of the Vale of Leven District Council, the Helensburgh District Council, the Dumbarton Burgh Council and the Helensburgh Burgh Council; 1 member and 1 official nominated by Cove and Kilcreggan Burgh Council and representatives of the Scottish Arts Council and the Scottish Sports Council. The local authorities represented, with the exception of the County Education Committee, were to merge to form the Dumbarton District in the impending reorganisation of local government in Scotland in 1975. The Board was chaired by Duncan Mills, chairman of the County Council's Further Education Sub-Committee and 1 of the County's 3 representatives, and the County also provided an honorary administrative officer and an honorary finance officer.

6   The Board considered the inclusion of other interests, but it was felt that it was already large enough. Instead, both to reflect the geographical character of the area and provide opportunities for local agencies and individuals to take part in the Experiment, 3 Neighbourhood Development Groups were set up covering Dumbarton, the Vale of Leven and Helensburgh, the last including the Rosneath peninsula between the Gareloch and Loch Long. Members of the Neighbourhood Groups were nominated by a wide range of interests, including arts and sports organisations, local industry, schools and local authorities (Youth and Community Service and Social Work Departments) the Roman Catholic Archdiocese and Dumbarton Presbytery. The Groups had powers of co-option and a degree of administrative and financial independence (see paragraph 10 below) but it was part of the structure that overall control of policy and expenditure should remain with the Advisory Board. To provide a link with the Board, 1 Board member sat on each Neighbourhood Group. There was no reciprocal arrangement, a feature of the organisation which was never fully accepted by the Neighbourhood Groups. It so happened, however, that the Helensburgh Neighbourhood Group elected the Advisory Board representative as their Group chairman and at a later stage the chairman of the Dumbarton Group was co-opted to the Advisory Board when the Board member originally appointed to the Group ceased to be able to attend.

7 The 3 Neighbourhood Groups were operative from September 1974 by which time the staff were also in post (see paragraphs 11 and 14). Generally, each met at monthly intervals and later they held a number of joint meetings. The Advisory Board met monthly. To speed up decisions on projects, deal with problems which developed during the action period and consider arrangements for continuing projects beyond the Experiment, the Board decided in the early months of 1975 to establish an Executive Committee with some delegated powers. The original intention was that this Committee should also have limited powers to initiate projects but in view of strong objections from the Neighbourhood Groups to a further decision-making group, this function was withdrawn.

8 Because of the longer period taken to set up the Dumbarton Experiment, it was agreed by the Central Sponsors that the action period should continue until August 1976. As had been originally foreseen, the Advisory Board had to be reconstituted in 1975 as a result of local government reorganisation. The former 5 local authorities now became the single Dumbarton District and the education services of Dunbartonshire were taken over by the Strathclyde Regional Council. The new Advisory Board set up in May 1975 included representatives from Dumbarton District Council and Strathclyde Regional Education Committee, some of whom came fresh to the Experiment. Continuity was achieved by co-opting members who had served on the previous Advisory Board. This enlarged the Board considerably. Members were also co-opted from various community interests, bringing the total membership to 28. All told, some 40 people were involved in the work of the Board in one way or another. Discussions were enlivened by the new members but the new Dumbarton District Council, faced with the need to make increasing economies as well as with problems of reorganisation, had much less sympathy with the aims of the Experiment than the previous local authorities. They decided against making any further financial contribution in the second year and were not prepared to support projects likely to entail ongoing expenditure. This sparked off differences of view between Advisory Board members and Sponsors and attracted conflicting local comments. It slowed down progress midway through the action year 1975/76 and resulted in the deferment, curtailment and eventual cancelation of part of the project programmes. Negotiations for ongoing arrangements were also much restricted.

Funding arrangements

9 The finance was worked out originally on the basis that local authorities would contribute 25 per cent and central sources 75 per cent. In the event, the County Education Committee and all but one of the local authorities originally represented contributed in the first year, the latter in amounts roughly proportionate to their populations. In the second year only the Regional Council contributed, bringing the total local authority contribution to £41,000. The Department of Education and Science contributed £100,000 (through the Scottish Arts Council) to the general fund,

the Scottish Education Department £70,000, the Scottish Sports Council £30,000 and the Department of the Environment £10,000 towards research costs. Altogether, and including some interest (contributions were paid periodically into a fund account), the funds available totalled £260,000.

10 Each of the 3 Neighbourhood Groups was authorised to operate independently within certain limits. Initially each was allocated £5,000 to undertake activities — later increased to £6,750 — and the cost of administration was met centrally, amounting to a further allocation which varied according to the kind of accommodation occupied. The Groups could fund projects costing up to £200 which they could select and carry through on their own authority. This was later increased to £500. Projects costing more could be considered and recommended for approval by the Advisory Board (or its Executive). In practice and as a matter of expediency, the Groups could examine projects up to £1,000 but these needed to have the approval of the Advisory Board.

Staffing, offices and co-ordination

11 The professional staff appointed reflected the local structure. An Area Co-ordinator was appointed to serve each of the 3 Neighbourhood Groups with a Project Director leading the team. These staff appointments with clerical support were completed by September 1974. Other staff were taken on during the period for individual projects or to develop activities in particular parts of the District. Arrangements for evaluation were made with the Area Survey Unit of Strathclyde University and the Evaluator took up his post in October of that year.

12 Board meetings were held on local authority premises but the Experiment was co-ordinated from premises in College Street rented originally from Dumbarton Burgh Council. Some supporting services were provided by Dunbartonshire County Council and after reorganisation were shared between Strathclyde Regional Council and Dumbarton District Council. The College Street premises also served as the base for the Dumbarton Neighbourhood Group whilst the Helensburgh and Vale of Leven Neighbourhood Groups established their office centres locally — the former in the Old Police Station at Helensburgh and the latter in a converted shop in Alexandria (Vale of Leven).

13 The Director's co-ordinating role brought him in touch with all groups and projects. Generally he was concerned with administration and negotiation rather than the details of projects, but the main contacts which most of the project organisers had with the Experiment were through the Director or the Area Co-ordinators. Additionally, the Director had powers, in consultation with the Chairman of the Advisory Board, to authorise minor projects with expenditure up to £100.

14   Each of the 3 Area Co-ordinators was assigned to a Neighbourhood Group, but had a 'subject role' as well. The Area Co-ordinator for Dumbarton Neighbourhood Group was responsible for the arts content of the overall Experiment programme, the Area Co-ordinator for Helensburgh for sports activities and the Vale of Leven Co-ordinator covered environmental aspects. In the latter part of the Experiment there were only 2 Area Co-ordinators and their District-wide subject responsibilities tended to become more important then their area functions. The Area Co-ordinators were in many ways the key links in the structure of the Dumbarton Experiment. They encouraged or organised specific projects, they played an effective part in influential sub-groups (such as the Arts Working Group), serviced the Neighbourhood Groups, and attended the Advisory Board. They acted as filters through which grass roots ideas for projects were put to the Neighbourhood Groups and Advisory Board, and through which decisions of these bodies were interpreted to local people.

15   The 3-fold geographical divisions of the District coupled with the degree of autonomy given to each Neighbourhood Group tended to promote the element of rivalry already mentioned as existing in the previous local government structure, rather than encourage a coordinated drive over the whole District. Nevertheless, in the latter part of the Experiment, the Groups began at their joint meetings to consider what might be attempted by concerted action or to give support to projects undertaken by a particular Neighbourhood Group. A cross flow of participation began to take place. Examples of this included an Athletics Event sponsored by the Dumbarton Neighbourhood Group and the Conference on Alcoholism, sponsored by the Vale of Leven Neighbourhood Group.

Programme approach

16   The basis for the Advisory Board's programme of action was a document based on the terms of reference prepared by an official of the Dunbartonshire County Education Department. The aim of the Experiment was to 'offer opportunities for cultural enrichment in the broad areas of the arts and sport' accepting that 'all that anyone can do is to attempt to dispel prejudice and suspicion, attempt to stir interest and thereafter offer practical possibilities. If people can be assisted to try something new and to do it for its own sake and not the subsidiary "good" it will do them, then cultural enrichment becomes a possibility.'

17   The criteria adopted by the Board for projects laid stress upon coordinating and extending the scope and quality of activities already present; providing opportunities for participation to a wider section of the community; and offering possibilities of continued and progressively improved activities. In this Experiment, the Evaluator, who was in post from October 1974, maintained a detached role, designing and carrying out a programme of project evaluation independent of the Advisory Board, Neighbourhood Groups and Experiment Team. Evaluation

aspects therefore played no part in framing and agreeing decisions on projects. Nor was there any systematic feedback from the evaluation. Nevertheless the Evaluator maintained constant contact with all parts of the Experiment and his reports were circulated widely. In time he became rather more involved though his independence was never in doubt.

First action

18   In the first 6 months administration of the Experiment was carried out by an official of the Dunbartonshire Youth and Community Service. An early task was to publicise the start of the Experiment. This was done by news items on Radio Clyde (the local commercial radio station) and BBC Scotland. Press releases were issued to the local media and articles were published in the Scottish national press. From the first ideas received, a number of projects were put in hand within the first few months in order to arouse wider interest. These early projects included assistance to various schemes already at the planning stage, for example, summer playschemes, family days at sports centres, a canoe project at Bowling, and events at the Vale of Leven Gala Day, one of which led to the formation of an archery club for the area. Full scale action on projects was, however, held over until the Director and his 3 assistants had been appointed and were in post. The main programme of projects got under way early in 1975, about a year after the first meeting.

19   After staff were appointed and Neighbourhood Groups set up, it was again necessary to renew the initial publicity. A series of meetings with arts and sports representatives had been held for the purpose of electing representatives on the Neighbourhood Groups and once these had met each held a further series of open meetings in an attempt to gather ideas. Some were well attended, others not. They were coupled with further publicity through the local press and other media. The Experiment Team prepared a Quality of Life News Sheet at roughly 2-month intervals. In the latter half of the Experiment a full time Publicity Officer continued these activities, continuing the News Sheet in a revised form. Other ideas were generated by working groups, and contacts with the Education and Social Work departments. Since the Area Co-ordinators also had subject responsibilities this too had an obvious influence on the pattern of the programme. Additionally the Experiment Team carried out an intensive survey of all organisations within the District who were concerned with leisure, as a means of trying to find out where gaps in the provision existed. The survey was subsequently published in the form of a Leisure Guide.

Handling the projects

20   Each project was considered by the Experiment Team as a whole, then investigated by a team member. If it was thought to be viable, a report was prepared. Projects were considered by one or more Neigh-

bourhood Groups before, in the case of major projects, they were submitted to the Advisory Board or its Executive Committee. Consideration and approval generally took 2 weeks, and rarely more than 4. At a later stage 'assessment' reports were prepared by the team for projects and groups of projects, as well as the evaluation reports written by the Evaluator.

21   Projects were organised in a number of different ways: by individuals, through existing clubs, jointly with official bodies, or by working groups. Many projects were interlinked.

22   Two outstanding characteristics of the programme of projects in the Dumbarton Experiment were the almost bewildering diversity of the activities sponsored and the low cost of most of them. This was due in part to the financial conditions under which the Neighbourhood Groups worked but also reflected what the Advisory Board thought was right for the area. Of the 163 projects in which the Experiment gave some financial assistance, only 14 involved sums exceeding £2,000. The total of £88,600 for these 14 projects was 64 per cent of the total project funds available. The programme included projects for drama, music, film and cine, video, arts development, poetry, screen printing; for a wide range of sports including those using the water facilities and mountains of the area; for outdoor recreation and indoor activities; for children, young people, families and the elderly; and for the disadvantaged including the physically disabled, blind and partially sighted, unemployed teenagers, young offenders and children in care.

The projects

23   The Experiment adopted a classification of major and minor projects. The Neighbourhood projects were regarded as minor ones, i.e. mostly under £500. Where projects cost more, were common to more than one Neighbourhood or were District-wide, they would be regarded as major District projects wholly or partly financed by the Advisory Board. There were also some minor projects initiated by the Advisory Board which were District-wide. Of the 163 projects implemented (in this Experiment each cost allocation counted as 1 project) there were 35 District major, 9 District minor projects and the 3 Neighbourhood Groups undertook a total of 119 — Dumbarton 31, Helensburgh 50 and Vale of Leven 38.

24   Of the major District projects the largest included an Arts Bus — a double decker bus converted to make a mobile arts centre (miniature theatre, cinema, exhibition space, equipment for discos and record recitals) which visited various sites within the area. A 3-month Community Drama project was carried out by a professional company — the 7:84 Theatre Company from Glasgow — engaged to live in the District, write dramatic entertainment based on local history, also using local material, and to tour village halls, social clubs and leisure centres. To encourage interest in writing and literature a Literary Group Tour was

arranged, again for a 3-month period. The poet Tom Buchan supported by other writers and artists visited pubs, community centres, hospitals and other places, giving informal readings and encouraging writers' workshops. These workshops were developed later in the Experiment and the Workers Education Association started a writers class. The Arts Working Group and Arts Co-ordinator took a leading part in developing these as well as many smaller arts projects. Other District-wide projects included a network of Mother and Toddler Groups which eventually formed their own association; Summer Playschemes were extended into areas where none previously existed including some rural areas; a land line was put in to extend the Hospital Broadcasting Service; a Poetry competition was run by a local newspaper; Guided Walks were organised to places of interest, leading to the formation of a new hill walking club; and support was given to the Bellsmyre festival in Dumbarton.

25   Some projects promoted by individual Neighbourhood Groups drew in people from a much wider catchment area and became combined District and Neighbourhood schemes. The Denny Arts Festival was a 2-week programme of events partly to demonstrate the potential for making greater use of the Civic Theatre in Dumbarton. Plays, exhibitions and musical events were staged in the theatre and open air events put on in the Town Square. Also in Dumbarton the Overtoun project aimed to develop a Victorian mansion house and its grounds for both arts and sports activities. A number of events were arranged in the house including exhibitions, and visits by old people. It also served as a base for the Community Drama project and as a centre for a number of activities developed in the grounds — musical performances, natural history, community fireworks and guided walks. The major cost of this project was borne by the Advisory Board but running costs were met by Dumbarton District Council who owned the premises and Dumbarton Neighbourhood Group provided some equipment and supported a number of the events. The use of Overtoun House had long been a problem with Dumbarton Burgh Council; its future became a controversial issue again in the last year of the Experiment when to the disappointment of the Neighbourhood and Overtoun Development Groups Dumbarton District — mainly because of costs — decided to close the house from April 1976, although some activities were allowed to continue in the grounds. A further project (Vale of Leven) started with a Conference on Alcoholism, a growing problem in the area and locally 'considered to be significant to the quality of life'. This attracted support from a great many sectors of Dumbarton and led to the setting up of a Council on Alcoholism for the District.

26   A further Neighbourhood project which developed into one of some complexity and was unique to this Experiment was the Video (Community Television) scheme, later known as Cablevision. This was based in the Vale of Leven Experiment Centre. Starting with the appointment of a professional worker to develop the community use of video, courses were arranged for individuals and groups, and the equipment

was available for loan. Sports clubs were particularly interested in the potential of video. But it was the later development of this project which involved many in its organisation and aroused interest beyond the Experiment area. A local cable television company provided the opportunity for a 6-week experiment in broadcasting using video tapes made by local people. The Experiment was granted a temporary licence to broadcast by the Home Office and the project was carried out under the direction of a Steering Committee and production team working in co-operation with the Scottish Film Council and the cable company. Producing the tapes and working to a rigid timetable provided an exacting and stimulating experience for all who took part. Individual tapes mostly made by small groups of 5 to 6 but others involved 20 to 30 people. The number of potential viewers was limited since not all homes were on the cable circuit or could get the particular channel used. Some people were critical of the technical quality of programmes and, according to surveys, of the cable system itself but there was support for a permanent service with local interest and increased awareness of the community.

27   The provision of an information service based on the central and neighbourhood offices was an important feature of this Experiment. Comprehensive information about organisations was compiled by the Director and his team and maintained throughout the period. News of the Experiment and of other events was disseminated regularly through various publicity methods and local press. A complete photographic record of the Experiment was made.

28   The Advisory Board instituted a system of transport grants to enable clubs and societies to enjoy cultural, social and other events and develop their activities more fully. The system was also supported by the Neighbourhood Groups. Although advertised regularly the project was not pushed; fewer people than expected took advantage of the grants.

29   Many organisations throughout the District were helped to extend their activities by the provision of Central Pools of Equipment. There were, in fact, 3 'pools' — 1 for arts activities, 1 for sports equipment for a range of activities, e.g. athletics, archery, weight training and 1 with items for general purpose use such as portable seating and public address systems. Although the concept of having a central pool of equipment stemmed from the Advisory Board and items were purchased as minor District projects, many items were provided on the initiative of Neighbourhood Groups. This was part of the help all the Neighbourhood Groups, in one form or another gave to a very wide range of existing organisations. In addition to aid with equipment, the Groups helped towards organising events, assisted with administration and publicity, gave guarantees against loss for some projects and improved premises and facilities in many cases where for one reason or another the organisation had not qualified for grant from other sources. Clubs were encouraged to help themselves, some by means of loans. Inaugural

grants between £10 and £500 were given to help establish new clubs and develop new interests.

30   Among the projects specifically related to individual Neighbourhood areas were those in which professionals were engaged to work within local communities. Two of these were concerned with deprived areas within the Vale of Leven. A Community Worker in Renton helped an existing community action group to establish an information shop and a community newspaper, as well as stimulating interest in other activities and encouraging improvement of the environment in a locality prone to vandalism. Another activist developed an Intermediate Treatment Scheme for young offenders. In Helensburgh a 'Creative Activist' was appointed to develop artistic activities within a housing estate lacking leisure facilities; lack of local acceptance meant that this particular activist was never able to establish his work effectively.

31   It is impossible in a short summary such as this to do justice to the full range of minor projects which were undertaken by the 3 Neighbourhood Groups. Some have already been mentioned and named; for the rest the project titles themselve give an indication of the variety. They include, for example, in Dumbarton: a children's theatre, a new string ensemble, a hockey international, an open event for non-athletes, a town trail; in Helensburgh: a toy making competition, a new craft club for the blind, a youth club run by young people in a rural area, a rock concert, a feasibility study of an open air pool due for closure, a table tennis marathon; in the Vale of Leven: a local history, a town map, tape recorded stories for old people in hospital, help for the Haldane choir and for the improvement of Community Education Centre facilities.

32   In the latter stages of the Experiment the Neighbourhood Groups began to combine and share in a number of projects. One such project was Informal Music Making — the provision of a supply of sheet music held in a local library but available for loan throughout the District. All Neighbourhoods, too, came together in a 2-day Decathlon event. Although this was financed as a minor District project, with the Helensburgh Neighbourhood Group providing the trophy, it involved a range of clubs with events staged in all parts of the District.

The future of projects and activities

33   Financial difficulties towards the end of the Experiment meant that neither the Strathclyde Region nor the Dumbarton District were in the terms of the Advisory Board's final report 'in a position to help in a direct way but specific help had been offered in continuing certain projects through the Urban Aid Programme and through the Manpower Services Commission'. The projects to be continued by these means were generally those with social content, for example the Community Worker and Shop was to continue with Urban Aid. It was hoped that the Manpower Services Commission Job Creation Programme would

enable other projects to be carried on in some form or other — the Arts Bus for example, now taken over by the District Council and the development of community video under the aegis of the Arts Working Group which planned to continue to promote arts projects using an old church hall as their base. It was also hoped that the newly established Local Sports Council would be prepared to extend and develop the work of the Experiment.

34   On a more positive note, the Equipment Pool was to be continued with responsibility divided between the District and Regional Councils, voluntary organisations continuing to have the use of items. For many projects, however, it proved impossible to make arrangements which would provide effectively for their continuance beyond the Experiment end. Interest was aroused but how much will have been sustained cannot be measured at this stage. No arrangements were made to continue the Advisory Board in any form but at the request of the Neighbourhood Groups the Regional Community Education Service were to be approached to see if they could be used in some form or other. The Helensburgh Group arranged in any event to reconvene in December 1976 after the Experiment had finished to discuss whether they could as individuals play a useful part in the community in the future.

Dumbarton Experiment

Summary of projects (for fuller details see Paper 3 in Volume 2)

Ref. No.	Name of Project	Summary Description	Cost to Experiment £
1	**Apiary**	V Apiary provided in major public park. Three open days held.	234
2	**Apollo Players**	D Four performances by visiting amateur Theatre Company from Glasgow.	150
3	**Archery Club**	V Archery Club established in Community Education Centre.	(included in project 67)
4	**Arts Bus**	Mobile Centre for a variety of arts projects in a converted double decker bus. Bus used for films, puppet shows, theatre groups, crafts, discos, etc.	15,438
5	**Arts Facilities**	V Development of an Arts Facilities Centre in an old church hall (to be converted) to serve as base for the Dumbarton and District Arts Working Group (see project 6).	1,000
6	**Arts Working Group**	Establishment of an Arts Charitable Trust Group to continue after the Experiment.	899
7-22	**Assisted Events**	Support for single or series of events including visit from professional orchestra, local orchestral and choral concerts, youth club discos, sports clubs marathons, community galas, carnivals, games week, neighbourhood week, town fireworks, sampling an art.	2,404
23	**Athletics for Everyone**	D Sport for the non-athletic — an evening event — to take part in track and field events.	265

NOTES:

(1) The letters D V H (Dumbarton, Vale of Leven, Helensburgh) indicate where projects were approved wholly or in part by a particular Neighbourhood Group and/or took place in a particular Neighbourhood.

(2) Costs in the Experiment are in gross terms and, pending final financial details which were not available at the time of writing, were based on the final local report to the Local Group.

Ref. No.	Name of Project	Summary Description	Cost to Experiment £
24	**Bellsmyre Festivals 1974, 1975**	**D** Annual festivals in a Neighbourhood Estate: range of events — theatre, folk concert, school show, football competition. Repeat of one held in 1973 without financial help.	1,711
25	**Botanical Survey**	**H** Botanical survey of local urban areas — to gather information under expert guidance. Open to anyone.	30
26	**Cablevision**	Six Weeks Broadcasting programme — a development of the video project. (see project 162).	4,200
27	**Cafe Disco, Rosneath (Phoenix Club)**	**H** Cafe cum disco club for teenagers set up to provide meeting place in a village lacking opportunities for young people.	150
28	**Canal Project, Bowling**	**D** A canoe store in a converted railway bridge arch. Proposal to clear stretch of canal and develop a canoeing centre; linked later with proposal to provide a picnic area.	860
29	**Children's Theatre**	**D** Scheme of drama for young people under an appointed leader. Some 70 children initially interested.	311
30	**Children's Wall and Ground Games**	Visually attractive games on walls and ground in playgrounds, both public and in schools.	500
31	**Cine Club Film**	**D** Help to Club to make documentary film of process in local firm.	100
32-48	**Club Equipment**	Help to individual clubs with purchase of equipment to enable them to continue and develop. Clubs were not otherwise eligible for grant aid from other sources.	3,450
49-53	**Club Equipment (pooled)**	Purchase of equipment which was available for loan by clubs; to enable clubs to develop activities including athletics, cine, cycling, skiing. (See also projects 67-69).	2,692
54	**Community Development Worker, Renton**	**V** Appointment of Community Development Worker to work on a particular housing estate.	3,415

Ref. No.	Name of Project	Summary Description	Cost to Experiment £
55	**Community Drama**	A 4-week tour by the 7:84 Theatre Company (Scotland) giving performances in community meeting places.	6,290
56	**Community Education Centre Improvement**	**V** Grant towards moveable partition to improve facilities for club meetings.	605
57	**Community Information Shop**	**V** A Community Information Shop provided in a converted launderette, used as an information service, casual meeting place, and also as an office for a Community Development Worker.	467
58	**Community Newspaper, Dumbarton**	**D** Support to group of local writers to set up a community newspaper, and produce 3 editions, subject to revision after each edition and to the group getting legal advice.	160
59	**Community Newspaper, Renton**	**V** Support given for further development of a community newspaper.	165
60-61	**Conference and Council on Alcoholism**	Conference on Alcoholism held and Council set up. The Experiment met cost and assisted with initial running costs.	1,447*
62	**Creative Activist**	**H** A Creative Activist appointed to live and work in selected neighbourhood.	3,643
63	**Decathlon Event**	Two day sports event organised by joint effort in all 3 neighbourhoods.	240
64	**Denny Arts Festival**	**D** Two week Arts Festival with a range of events, and using the local civic theatre more intensively — plays, exhibitions, music, poetry, rock groups and cabaret produced.	6,674
65	**Design a Toy Competition**	**H** An adult toy design and children's painting competition and exhibition. National toy firm judged competition and manufactured winning toy.	45
66	**Environment Conference**	One day Conference to discuss environmental issues.	230

Ref. No.	Name of Project	Summary Description	Cost to Experiment £
67-69	**Equipment Pools**	Central pools of sport, art and other equipment to help develop activities. Items including portable seating, public address system, stage lighting, exhibition stands, electric organ etc., were available on loan.	8,600
70-72	**Exhibitions**	Promotion of 2 art exhibitions and assistance given to a third: Children's Art; W of Scotland Artists tour; John Logie Baird.	20 (project 70 only)
73	**Family Days at Garelochhead**	H Attempt to develop casual use of Outdoor Education Centre. Opportunities for sailing, canoeing, cycling, fishing, hill walking.	(included in project 135)
74	**Feasibility Study — Outdoor Swimming Pool**	H Feasibility study into future use of an outdoor swimming pool which was being superseded by new indoor pool.	200
75	**Federation of the Arts**	H Attempt to form Federation of Arts with a view to obtaining better accommodation.	(included in Experiment Administration.)
76	**Floodlighting Facilities: Posties Park**	Provision of foundation for floodlighting of a football pitch and running track and some equipment.	6,700
77	**Floodlighting Facilities: Rugby Football Club**	D Improvement of training facilities by floodlighting school playing surface.	500
78	**Guided Walks**	Walks with specialist leaders arranged in all parts of the District — archaeology, ornithology, geology, etc.	190
79	**Haldane Film Society**	V New equipment to improve standards. Club expanded work of providing specialist shows for voluntary groups.	965
80-84	**Help for Small Groups**	Help with duplicating service, stationery, printing and in 2 instances small grant towards rent to prevent closure.	277
85	**Hockey International**	D International hockey match staged on school pitch.	150

Ref. No.	Name of Project	Summary Description	Cost to Experiment £
86	**Hockey Tournament**	**H** Five-a-Side indoor hockey tournament for non Club members as part of local town celebration. Assistance also given to Club.	127
87	**Hospital Broadcasting**	**V** Extension of Hospital Broadcasting System by provision of land line.	629
88	**Hospital Broadcasting Seminar**	**D** Support for national conference to exchange ideas.	75
89	**Impact Youth Club Visit**	**V** Newly formed Youth Club given support to go on a cultural visit to London.	792
90-96	**Improvement of Facilities**	Help towards cost of improving facilities for clubs unable to obtain any or sufficient grant from other sources. Clubs helped included an Amenity Society, Girl Guides, Scouts, Golf, Rugby and Cricket; a Sports Centre and Parish Hall were also aided.	2,560
97	**Informal Music Making**	A library of music scores selected and made available in local library for individual music makers.	220
98	**Information Sevices**	An information service on organisations and leisure services, etc., maintained at the Experiment central office and neighbourhood centres.	(included in administrative costs of Experiment)
99	**Intermediate Treatment Scheme**	**V** Appointment of a Project Leader to develop activities for groups of delinquent children. Two groups established in the 1 year.	5,318
100	**Junior Arts, Renton**	**V** Latch key children given the chance to try craft activities with help of a leader/activist.	500
101	**Kilcreggan Music Project**	**H** Guitars and instruction provided for children in isolated rural area. Guitars used also by adults in evening classes.	750
102	**Kirkmichael Centre**	**H** Conversion of 2 houses adjoining playing field into a Centre/Pavilion.	315*

Ref. No.	Name of Project	Summary Description	Cost to Experiment £
103	**Kirkmichael Part Time Activist**	**H** A part time Activist appointed to develop activities in a housing estate lacking facilities.	200
104	**Kite Flying Competition**	A 'fly your home made kite' event.	30
105	**Literary Group Tour**	A 3 month tour of Dumbarton District by poet Tom Buchan with support from other writers and artists.	891
106	**Mother and Toddler Clubs**	Support for new and existing Mother and Toddler Clubs and formation of Development Group Association to co-ordinate work.	2,250
107	**Movement Festival**	A week of activities displaying movement involving a number of local clubs.	503
108-126	**New Clubs**	Inaugural grants and help given in establishing new clubs in a variety of art and sport acitivies, and for children, for youth and for the blind. (Other new clubs listed in projects 3 and 27.)	1,964
127-130	**New Community Action Groups**	Limited support in setting up new action groups — contribution to initial expenses.	195
131	**Operetta at Primary School**	Help with equipment for performance at a primary school.	66
132	**Optimum Use of School Sports Facilities**	Pilot 10 week scheme to promote weekend use of local school sports facilities. Scheme started January 1976.	823
133	**Overtoun House**	**D** The development of a Victorian Mansion and its ground as a facility for arts and sports activities. House gifted to the District Council in 1939.	13,150*
134	**Photographic Record**	A photographic record of the Experiment by part time Photographer, later full time.	3,750
135	**Pick-a-Sport and Take-a-Part-in-Art**	**V** Opportunities to try forms of art and sport arranged as part of Gala Week.	625*

Ref. No.	Name of Project	Summary Description	Cost to Experiment £
136	**Poetry Competition**	**H** Local newspaper ran a District-wide competition — a pilot scheme for 3 weeks for 3 age groups.	144*
137-142	**Publications**	Encouragement given to writers by giving support to publications. These included 2 on local history, rights of way and leisure guides and a writers' group publication.	3,815
143	**Publicity and Publicity Officer**	Experiment with various methods of publicity. Appointment of Publicity Officer in last year of Experiment.	15,286
144	**Quality of Life Conference**	**D** A public conference to discuss concept of the quality of life.	127
145	**Rock Concert**	**H** A Rock Concert organised by young people for young people held in largest hall in Helensburgh.	1,098
146	**Sailing**	Series of meetings to try and form Community Sailing Association of local authority providers, sailing clubs and interested individuals.	(included in Experiment Administration.)
147	**Sports Activist: 'Its Your Street Scheme'**	Full time Worker appointed to promote community participation in sports activities by bringing sport to the people.	1,000
148-153	**Summer Playschemes**	Extension of Summer Playschemes into areas lacking such schemes. Schemes in 1974 in all 3 Neighbourhoods. Two supported in 1975 and 1 in 1976.	850*
154	**Survey of Play Facilities**	Survey of 'What Children thought of their Play Facilities'. Children sent in comments, ideas, drawings, poems.	Included in Experiment Administration.
155	**Talking Newspaper**	**H** A tape recorded newspaper for the blind and partially sighted. Equipment purchased and administrative help given.	140
156	**Tape Recordings for Geriatric Hospital Patients**	**V** Extension of an existing service by provision of new equipment and voluntary recording.	207

Ref. No.	Name of Project	Summary Description	Cost to Experiment £
157	**Theatre Workshop for the Elderly**	**D** Group of elderly people attended workshop performance by a West London Theatre Company.	70
158	**Town Map**	**V** The preparation of a Town Map showing places of interest (in lieu of town trail — see following project).	100
159	**Town Trail**	**D** Two students of architecture devised Town Trail in Dumbarton. Research also completed for trail in Helensburgh.	300
160	**Transport Grants**	Provision of transport grants to assist sports clubs, amenity societies, social and recreational activities. Vale of Leven additionally gave support to a school excursion.	1,832
161	**Vale Folk Songs**	**V** Songs written by local song writer reproduced.	100
162	**Video (Community Television)**	Promotion of the use of video by individuals and groups. Activist appointed.	2,543
163	**Writers' Workshop**	Writers' workshops set up following a number of public meetings, and the Literary Group tour.	(included in Experiment Administration)
		Total gross expenditure on projects	**139,722**

Note. *Money was also made available by other agencies towards the overall costs.

Printed in England for Her Majesty's Stationery Office by Croydon Printing Company Limited, Croydon, Surrey.

Dd. 587564 K20 6/77